SHORT CIRC...

IN THE PEAK ...

PAT AND PETER TIDSALL

28 WALKS OF 3 TO 6 MILES

Follow the Countryside code

1) Be safe and plan ahead and follow any signs
2) Keep dogs under control
3) Prevent uncontrolled moorland fires
4) Protect plants and animals, take your litter home
5) Leave gates and property as you find them
6) Consider other people
7) Beware mineshafts! Derbyshire alone has over 100,000 mine shafts. Keep away from depressions in the ground in the mining areas of the Peak District. Several of the walks in this book pass through mining areas, so stay on rights of way at all times.

Published by **Ashbourne Editions**
Ashbourne Hall, Cokayne Ave
Ashbourne, Derbyshire, DE6 1EJ England
Tel: (01335) 347349 Fax: (01335) 347303
e-mail: landmark@clara.net

13 ISBN: 978 1 873775 27 1

Printed by: Cromwell Press Ltd, Trowbridge

Design & reproduction by: Michelle Prost

Acknowledgements: The author wishes to thank Roma Wilcock for her
company and help in updating these walks.

Front cover: Biggin Dale
Back cover: Beresford Dale in winter
Opposite page: Cave Dale

SHORT CIRCULAR WALKS

IN THE PEAK NATIONAL PARK

PAT AND PETER TIDSALL

28 WALKS OF 3 TO 6 MILES

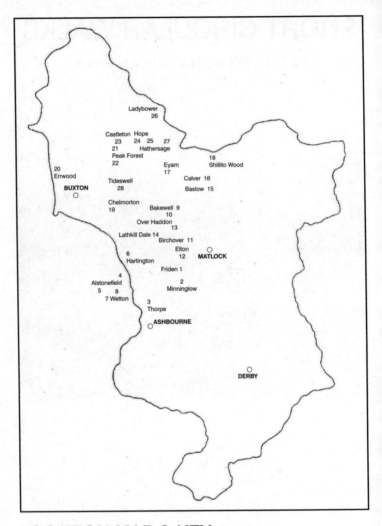

Ladybower
26

Castleton Hope
23   24 25   27
21   Hathersage
Peak Forest
22   18
            Eyam   Shillito Wood
            17
20
Errwood   Calver 16
BUXTON   Tideswell
○   28   Baslow 15

Chelmorton
19   Bakewell 9
                10
          Over Haddon
                13
Lathkill Dale 14
          Birchover 11
        6   Elton
    Hartington   12   MATLOCK
                          ○
          Friden 1
        4
Alstonefield   2
5   8   Minninglow
7 Wetton
        3
      Thorpe
      ○ ASHBOURNE
      ○

                    ○
                  DERBY

LOCATION MAP & KEY (OPPOSITE)

All the walks start at recognised car parks unless stated otherwise in
the detailed walk descriptions.

Hanging Stone

	Roads			Woods
	Tracks: Drives			Rock Outcrops
	Railways		⊞	Church
	Trails		▲	Youth Hostel
	The Route		F.B.	Footbridge
	Rivers		C.P.	Car Park
	Lakes		P.H.	Public House: Inns

WALK INDEX

WALK INDEX

This book of short circular walks is very adaptable being suitable for first time walkers, people visiting the Peak District and also for walkers who wish to do only a half-day walk.

By the very nature of the area all walks will have hills of varying length and steepness. Although they are short walks they are not necessarily easy.

The grades refer only to the total height climbed in each walk. Please bear in mind that all descriptions are relative to the Peak District.

1. Grades 1: less than 300ft [91 metres]

2. Grade 2: 300ft to 600ft [91 metres to 183 metres]

3. Grade 3: 600ft. to 1000ft [183 metres to 305 metres]

Other information provided:-

1 * These indicate difficult sections of the route, such as ascents, descents or terrain.

2. Stiles:- S – 1 to 10, SS – 10 to 20, SSS – over 20

3. The distance is given to the nearest half mile

4. The approximate time is for reasonably fit walkers and does not allow for stops. It is estimated that the average walking time is 2 miles per hour.

5. The two maps recommended for these walks are: Explorer OL24 and OL1

6. Parking is given with the Grid Ref. and in most cases is at a public car park. This is the start of the walk. On a few walks you may have to park on the roadside or in a layby. Please ensure that gates and roads are not blocked and other vehicles can pass safely.

7. Refreshment and picnic places are suggested but please bear in mind that they are not recommendations as the former can change hands and picnic areas may change. If you do picnic please take all litter away with you.

Walks 1, 2, 3, 7, 9, 10, 13, 15 and 20 all have short stretches that are wheel-chair and pushchair friendly.

The "Peak District AZ Visitor's Map" and the "Peak District & Derbyshire" Tour maps are useful for locating the starting points of the walks. Please take adequate protection against the changeable weather conditions and the terrain, we strongly recommend walking boots as parts of Derbyshire can be very muddy after rain. The higher you climb the lower the temperatures and often the stronger the winds.

The countryside is not static and changes may have taken place between the research for these walks and their publication. For example field boundaries, gates and gateways, diversions round farmyards, signs and waymarks, stiles, signposts and paths may have altered, as well as the uses of land and buildings.

Please note that the directions in the route instructions are given as you stand with your back to the stile or gate.

WALK 1

Friden and The Pennine Bridleway

Friden Trail Car Park and picnic area, Long Dale, A5012, Mouldridge Lane, Minninglow Car Park, Pennine Bridleway.

Map: Explorer OL 24 White Peak
Parking: Grid Ref. SK 172 607
Distance: 6$\frac{1}{2}$ Miles
Approx Time: 3 Hours
Grade: 1
Paths: Trails, minor roads and field paths
Stiles: S
Picnic: Instruction 5
Wheel Chair: Instructions 8 and 9

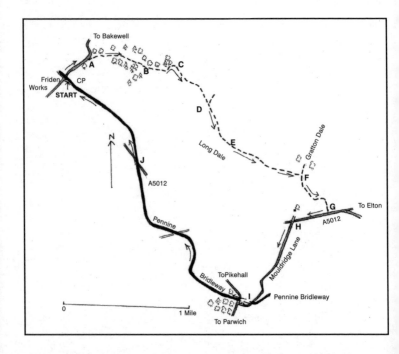

Directions

From Ashbourne take the A515 Buxton road and in about 10 miles turn right at Newhaven onto the A5012 and in 250 metres turn left along the Youlgreave road. In about ¼ mile turn right to the Friden car park

Description

A very pleasant walk along the less well known Long Dale [part of English Nature], where you will have wide open views above the dale and ideal picnic spots on a fine autumn day. As it is a bridleway, the upper reaches of the dale can be quite muddy after heavy rain. The total length of Long Dale to the junction with Gratton Dale is 2miles. The return route follows The High Peak Trail [now called the Pennine Bridleway] for 2 ½ miles.

The Trail from Friden car park to Minninglow car park is wheelchair and pushchair friendly. This section of the walk is also suitable for people wanting a short flat walk.

Route Instructions

1. From the car park return to the road and turn right. Walk down the road for about ¼ mile. You will go round a left hand bend and before you reach a right hand bend leave the road, at the Bridleway sign. {A} Follow this path down to and through a gate.

2. Continue ahead along a grassed walled track, which soon bends round to the left and then a little further on opens out into a wider walled and wooded area.

3. Cross the stile by the gate ahead and keep straight on. {B} At the end of the wood follow the wall and wood round to the left. Walk up out of the dale and near the top of the short rise turn right through a small gate. [Access Land] {C}

4. Walk across the valley side with a wall on the left, where this wall turns up left keep straight on across the gorse covered valley side. This is a good picnic spot with open views down towards the southern edge of the Peak District.

5. {D} After about ¼ mile and on reaching a farm gate and a bridleway sign on your left bear off right to follow a wide grass path through the gorse as you gradually descend back to the dale bottom.

6. Go through the waymarked gate {E} and turn right to continue down the dale for another ¾ mile. [About 15 minutes]

7. Cross a stile by a gate and turn right. {F} [Gratton Dale goes off to the left] Follow the path up the dale to go through a gateway. Soon you will have a wall close on the right. Follow this wall round a right hand bend then on to the A5012 via a farm gate. {G}

8. Turn right up the road and in about 450 metres turn left up the minor road, {H} Mouldridge Lane, towards Parwich. In about ¾ mile, where the High Peak Trail [Pennine Bridleway] crosses the road, turn right through the Minninglow car park and keep straight on to the trail. {I}

9. You will now follow the High Peak Trail [Pennine Bridleway] for 2 ½ miles back to Friden. Ignore all side paths and tracks. About ¾ of the way along the trail you will cross the A5012. {J}

WALK 2

Minninglow, Nr Pikehall

Pennine Bridleway, Royston Grange, Minninglow Lane and car park.

Map: Explorer OL 24 White Peak
Parking: SK 194 581
Distance: 3 miles
Approx Time: 1 ½ hours
Grade: 1
Paths: Trail, field paths and minor roads
Stiles: S
Picnic: At the car park
Wheel Chair: Along the Pennine Bridleway

Directions

From Ashbourne take the A515 Buxton road and in about 10 miles at Newhaven turn right to follow the A5012. In 2 miles at Pikehall turn right along a minor road for about ¾ mile and immediately after passing under a bridge turn left to enter the car park and picnic area on the left.
Grid Ref SK194581.

Description

An easy walk along the trail, [which is suitable for wheel chairs] then across undulating fields and returning via tracks and quiet country lanes. It is advisable to follow this route after a period of dry weather as one short rutted track can become very muddy. The information plaque at the car park is well worth reading. The nearest refreshment

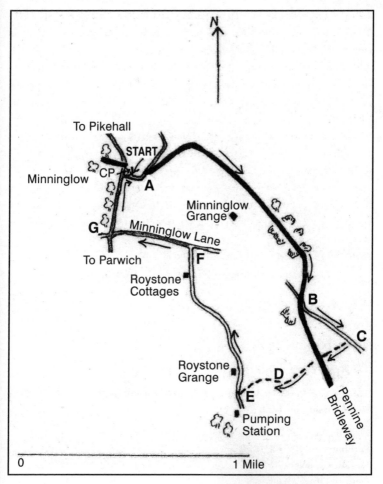

stops are at Grangemill 3 ½ miles further on along the A5012 from Pikehall towards Cromford, or down to Parwich.

Route Instructions

1. Leave the car park at the eastern gated end signed "Pennine Bridleway. Middleton Top 6½ miles". {A} Cross the road to follow the Pennine Bridleway for 1 mile [about 20 minutes].

2. Pass by a farm gate across the trail then bear off left to cross a stile by a gate. {B}

3. Follow the wide rutted walled track for just over ¼ mile and as you start to climb cross the wall stile on the right to Royston. {C}

4. Walk down the field to pass under the trail-bridge. Keep straight on down the next field aiming for a gateway and water trough. Go through the stile to the right of the gateway. Bear very slightly left to follow the wall on your left. Cross the stile on the left. {D}

5. Turn right down the farm track to pass through a gateway then keep a wall close on the right before crossing the gated stile on the right.

6. Bear left across the next field crossing the line of an old wall. Go over the wall stile and turn right. [Notice the pumping station over to the left] {E}

7. Walk up the surfaced drive through Royston Grange. Go through the gate and continue up the surfaced track for about ¾ mile passing through two more gates and Royston Cottages.

8. {F} Turn left up Minninglow Lane for about ¼ mile then turn right {G} for 400 metres before turning right again to the car park.

WALK 3

Thorpe and Tissington

Thorpe Car Park, Tissington Trail, Tissington Village, Peveril of the Peak Hotel, Tissington Trail.

Map: Explorer OL 24 White Peak
Parking: Grid Ref. SK 164 503
Distance: 5 miles
Approx Time: 2 hours
Grade: 1
Paths: Trail and field paths
Stiles: SSS
Refreshments: Dog and Partridge in Thorpe and The Coach House in Tissington. [Limited opening in the winter]
Wheel Chair: The Trail

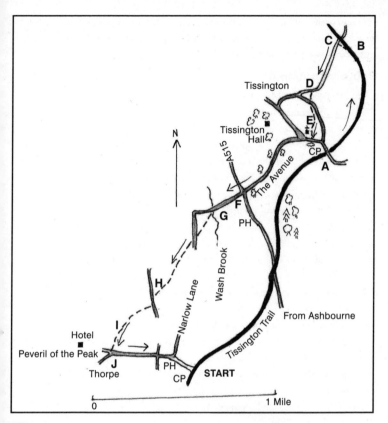

Directions

From Ashbourne take the A515 Buxton road. After about a mile turn left to Dovedale.
After another 2 miles at the Dog and Partridge in Thorpe turn right along Narlows
Lane for about 150 metres then turn right again down to the Tissington Trail Thorpe
car park.

Description

This is an easy walk following the Tissington Trail and field paths. You will be able to
visit the delightful village of Tissington, famous for its Well Dressing. Festival commenc-
ing on Ascension Day. The Coach House serves as a welcome refreshment break and
next to it is the attractive Tissington Hall. The trail from the Thorpe car park is wheel

chair and pushchair friendly. You can enjoy the 1½ miles to Tissington then return to the car park giving you a three-mile route. The Dog and Partridge in Thorpe is another refreshment stop at the end of the walk.

Route Instructions

1. With your back to the entrance to the car park turn left to follow the trail on the "Tissington 1 ½ miles" route.

2. After 1 ½ miles you will walk through Tissington car park. {A} Pass under the bridge to walk along the trail for another ¾ mile ignoring a long flight of steps on the left.

3. {B} Turn left to leave the trail at the sign " Public Footpath to Tissington and Parwich". Follow a wall on the left go through a small gate and turn left. {C}

4. Follow the lane for nearly ½ mile then cross a gated stile on the left. {D}

5. Bear slightly right across the field. Cross two stiles and the road. Keep straight on down the field to cross another stile in the bottom right-hand corner. Bear right across the next field and go through a gated stile into the churchyard. {E}

6. Keep a wall close on the left and turn left to go through a small metal gate. Walk down to the road. Turn right to pass the pond on the left.

7. Keep straight on up The Avenue to the main A515 road. {F}

8. Cross the road to walk down the minor road towards Dovedale. In about 300 metres turn left by a stream to go through a squeeze stile. {G}

9. Walk up the field bearing slightly right to cross a stile in the field corner. Cross the road to go through another squeeze stile.

10. Continue ahead crossing four fields and four stiles. In the fifth field bear slightly right to cross the stile by a farm gate, below Pike House. {H}

11. Turn left along the road for about 100 metres, then cross the stile on the right to follow the route to Thorpe.

12. Follow the wall on the right to cross a stile; now continue to follow the field boundary on the right for about 100 metres before crossing a squeeze stile on the right. {I}

13. Turn left to keep the field boundary close on the left. Go through two gates to enter the National Trust area. Keep the wall on the left until you reach a footpath post. Cross a stile on the left leaving the National Trust area.

14. Turn right across two fields and three stiles to reach the entrance to the Peveril of the Peak Hotel and the road. {J}

15. Turn left up the road for about ¼ mile. At the Dog and Partridge inn keep straight on along Narlow Lane for about 150 metres then turn right back to the car park.

WALK 4

Alstonefield

Alstonefield, Gipsy Bank, Wolfscote Dale, Narrow Dale, Alstonefield.

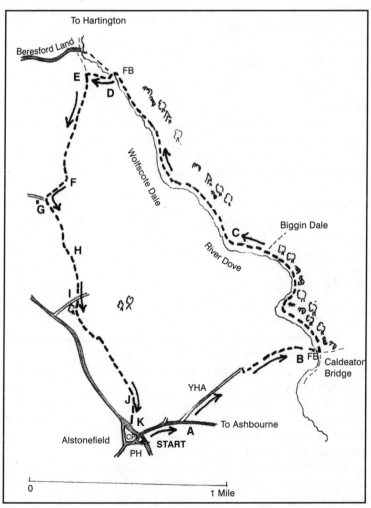

Map: Explorer OL 24 White Peak

Parking: Grid Ref. SK 131 556

Distance: 5 miles

Approx Time: 2 ¼ hours

Grade: 1★

Paths: Field and clear dale paths

Stiles: SSS

Refreshments: The George Inn, Alstonefield

Picnic: Along the Dale

Directions

From Ashbourne take the A515 Buxton road. In 5½ miles turn left to Alstonefield. Follow the minor road for nearly 3 miles crossing the River Dove. There are two car parks in the village, both clearly marked. The walk starts at The George Inn just off to the left as you enter the village. Grid Ref. SK131556.

Description

A walk of great contrasts where you follow upland field paths and tracks with wide open views and deep valley paths along the beautiful River Dove with steep limestone cliffs. The George inn is a pleasant refreshment stop.

Route Instructions

1. With your back to "The George" inn turn left to walk to the road then turn right follow the road to Ashbourne.

2. In about 400 metres turn left at the second track signed Youth Hostel. {A}

3. Follow the well-used track then path to the head of Gipsy Bank.

4. Cross the stile and bearing slightly right; walk down the very steep bank {B} to cross Coldeaton Bridge.

5. Turn left along the dale keeping the Dove on the left. After the second stile continue ahead along Wolfscote Dale with the Dove still on your left. {C} Two miles from Coldeaton Bridge you will cross a stile by The National Trust Sign. Immediately after crossing the stile turn left. {D}

6. Cross the footbridge to go through a gate and turn right. Follow the wide [new] path to go through another gate. Walk down to the track.

7. {E} Turn left ignoring the two gates on the right. Follow this track uphill. You will

cross stiles and gates.

8. In about ¾ mile the track turns sharp right uphill to go through a gate. {F} Walk up towards the buildings of Narrowdale, where you follow the track round to the left passing through two gates. {G}

9. Climb the wide grass track ahead, you will soon lose the wall on the right.

10. Continue keeping the wall on the left for a few metres then branch off up to the right away from the wall. {H}

11. Cross a wall stile ahead. Follow the wall now on your right to cross the stile in the field corner. Keep straight on across the next two fields and stiles. Cross the track to go through a small gate. {I}

12. Bear right to the wood corner and go through the gated stile. Turn left and follow a wall on the left to cross the stile ahead. Keep straight on passing a ruined breezeblock building. Cross the broken wall in the left hand field corner.

13. Keep a wall close on the right for a few metres then cross the stile on the right. Keep straight on crossing seven fields. In the eighth field follow a track round to the right then cross the stile on the left. {J}

14. Cross the field and stile ahead then bear right to cross another wall stile. Bear right again, first on a track, then across the field behind the houses. Cross the stile by the waymarked sign.

15. Turn right to walk down to the road via a gated stile. {K} Turn left to walk back to "The George" inn.

WALK 5

Alstonefield

Alstonefield, Gateham Farm, Wetton Hill, Wetton, Manifold Valley, Stanshope Lane, Hopedale, Alstonefield.

Map: Explorer OL 24 White Peak
Parking: SK 131 556
Distance: 6 miles
Approx Time: 3 hours
Grade: 2
Paths: Mainly clear field paths.
Stiles: SSS
Refreshments: The George in Alstonefield, The Royal Oak in Wetton and The Watts Russell in Hopedale [closed on Mondays].

Directions

From Ashbourne take the A515 Buxton Road. In 5 ½ miles turn left to Alstonefield. Follow the minor road for nearly 3 miles crossing the River Dove. There are two car parks in the village, both clearly signed. Grid Ref. SK131556. The walk will start at The George, which is clearly indicated off to the left as you enter the village.

Description

This is a delightful and varied walk from the pretty village of Alstonefield. The George Inn, where the walk starts, provides a welcoming and friendly refreshment stop. It is open all year round except on Christmas Day. The route follows field paths to Wetton, a small village of stone cottages, a number of them being for holiday renting.

Ye Olde Royal Oak in the centre of the village is a suitable refreshment stop. From here more field paths lead to the impressive edge of the Manifold Valley where there are wonderful views across the Staffordshire Peak District. The route returns to Alstonefield via Hopedale, a small hamlet with a delightful inn, The Watts Russell Arms [closed on Mondays].

Route Instructions

1. With your back to The George turn left to walk to the main village road and left again to follow the Hartington and Hulme End road which bends round to the right passing one of the car parks. Follow this road out of the village for nearly ½ mile pass-

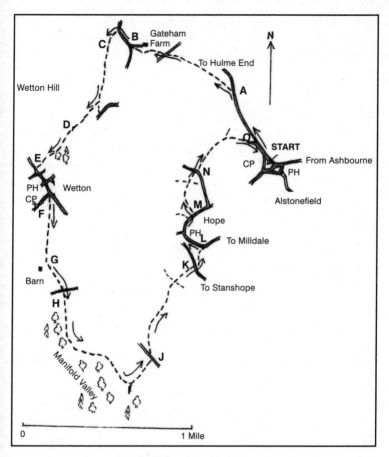

ing the derestriction and village signs.

2. {A} Cross the gated squeeze stile on the left and bear right across the field to cross another gated stile. Keep straight on to go through a third gated stile. In the next field pass the end of a broken wall and continue ahead across the undulating field, keeping a ditch down on the left. Go through two stiles ahead.

3. Keep straight on crossing two fields and two gated stiles. In the third field turn left through a stile nearly half way down the field. Bear right across the next field.

4. Cross the road via two stiles. Bear left down to the farm; go through a small gate by

the farm gate and cross the track. Pass Gateham Farm over to the right. Cross the wall stile then walk to the farm gate, cross the stile in the field corner onto the road.{B}

5. Turn right along the road for about 100 metres and where it bends right turn left over the stile and keep straight on to cross another stile into the National Trust area at Wetton.{C}

6. Bear left to a wall corner then follow the wall close on your left for 350 metres before turning left over the stile.{D}

7. Turn right to cross the stile ahead. Keep straight on crossing six fields and stiles. Walk through the top of a small wood, and then across a field and stile.

8. Bear right to cross a wall stile and turn left following the wall on the left to cross two fields and stiles onto the lane.{E}

9. Turn left down the lane then left again into Wetton. Pass the inn and at the road junction turn right signed "Grindon 2 ½ [Manifold Valley]. Almost immediately turn left.{F}

10. Walk up a short grassed walled track to cross a stile. Then cross the small field diagonally to cross another stile.

11. Bear left to cross two fields and stiles. In the third field bear left up to the narrow field corner to cross the wall stile near a small tree. Walk up towards a barn and as you near it bear left to cross the stile.{G}

12. Keep straight on down the field with the wall close on the right. Cross the road via two stiles.{H}

13. Follow the path ahead crossing a stile then turning right up to the footpath post and cross the stile.

14. You will now follow the path above the deep Manifold Valley for about ¾ mile.{I} You will cross one stile. After going through a small gate turn away from the valley up to a gate. [A good picnic spot]. Cross the stile by the gate.

15. Keep straight on following the "Hope Stanshope" route, which soon becomes a track with a wall on the left. Cross the road via two stiles.{J}

16. Bear left across the field and through the stile. Follow the walls on the left crossing three fields and stiles. In the fourth field at a wall corner bear slightly left to cross the stile in the field corner. Keep straight on to go through a small gate and keeping the wall on the right walk down to the road.{K}

17. Cross the road diagonally left to go through a stile. Walk down into the small dry valley and follow it down to the road. Go through a small gate and turn left along the road.{L}

18. Walk through the hamlet of Hope passing the inn and keeping straight on. At the

second footpath sign {M} turn left.

19. Follow a short grassy track to cross a stile. Keep straight on with the wall close on the right to cross two fields and gates. Immediately after the second gate go through a gated stile on the left, ignoring the stile and gate ahead.

20. Follow a slabbed path with a line of trees on the right. Cross the road via two small gates.{N}

21. Follow the wall on the left to cross a stile; you will now have the wall on the right as you cross two fields and small gates. Walk up the track to the main village road. Turn right back into Alstonefield. {O}

WALK 6
Hartington

Hartington Cheese Factory, Harris Close, Pilsbury, Bank Top Farm, Hartington.

Map: Explorer OL 24 White Peak
Parking: SK 127 362
Distance: 5 ¼ miles
Approx Time: 3 hours
Grade: 3★
Paths: Field and moorland paths.
Stiles: SSS
Refreshments: A number of refreshment facilities in Hartington including The Charles Cotton Hotel.
Picnic: Instruction 15.

Directions

From the A515, 11 miles north of Ashbourne, turn left to Hartington. Follow the B5054 for nearly 2 ½ miles to Hartington. There are two car parks, one in the centre of the village near the duck pond and a pay and display car park on the right of the B5054 as you drive out of the village towards Warslow. Grid Ref. SK 128364 and SK 127362 respectively.

Description

A varied and interesting walk with wonderful views eastward to the Derbyshire dales

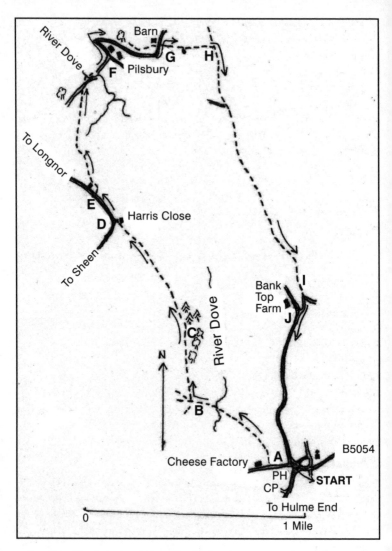

and south to Hartington and Dovedale. As there is a steep ascent and descent on to and down from the escarpment above the River Dove it would be advisable to follow this route after a period of dry weather. It has a fine 14th Century church that is well worth a visit. There are a number of refreshment facilities in the village, as well as the cheese shop linked to the Stilton cheese factory.

Route Instructions

1. The walk starts at the duck pond in the centre of the village. With the pond on your right walk along Stonewall Lane which leads to the Cheese Factory.

2. {A} Just before the factory turn right through a gate signed "Public Footpath to Sheen". Keep straight on to go through a gate and follow a path through the trees to go through another gate.

3. Cross the middle of the field and the stile ahead then bear left to cross the next stile. Bear slightly right across the next field to go through a squeeze stile.

4. Bear left downhill to go through the small gate then follow the hedge on your right for a short way before turning left over the footbridge.

5. Keep straight on up the field as directed to go through a small gate. {B} Turn right along the track for a few metres before crossing the stile on the left signed Harris Close.

6. Climb the steep hill ahead. Near the top bear round to the right passing the way marked post. Cross the stile into the pinewood. {C}

7. Follow the path through the wood. As you leave the wood continue ahead along the top of the escarpment with a wall close on the left. Cross a wall stile and bear right up the middle of the field passing a single tree on your right. Cross another stile at a wall corner.

8. Keep straight on to cross four stiles and four fields always heading for the farm.

9. Follow the narrow path by the farm buildings then pass in front of the Harris Close farmhouse and turn left to join the road. {D}

10 Turn right along the road for about 350 metres. {E} Cross a stile on the right by the footpath post then immediately cross a fence stile on the left. Bear right passing a house to cross the next stile. Turn left along a short fenced and walled path. Cross the stile ahead. Bear right across the hillside to and through a wall gap then through the stile ahead. Now follow the wall close on the left and round the field corner to go through a stile and gate.

11 Bear right downhill aiming for and passing a waymarked post. At the bottom of the hill go through a small gate onto a track. Turn right down the track. Cross the River Dove via a footbridge and turn right to join a track. Turn left up the track to a minor road in the small hamlet of Pilsbury. {F}

12 At this point you can turn right to follow the minor road for just over two miles

back to Hartington. [This would give you a 4 ¾ mile walk with less climbing] If you choose the 5 ¼ mile walk turn left.

13 Follow the minor road round Pilsbury and on up the hill. After nearly ½ mile turn right over a fence stile just before a barn on the left. {G}

14 Keep straight on to cross a broken wall then follow the path across open grassland, passing a stone and a waymarked post. On reaching a wall and a crossing of paths turn right to follow a wall close on the left up the steep field. {H}

15 Cross the gated wall stile and continue ahead across the undulating hillside passing three separate waymarked posts. Go through a gated stile by a farm gate and keep straight on to pass through a wide wall gap. Bear right down the field to go through a gate. The path now climbs up a short rocky gully before continuing to cross the hillside. In this next stretch you will cross two stiles and one wall gap. Continue ahead across a rocky area. Eventually there will be a wall close on the left and you will see Bank Top Farm down to the right. {I}

16 Go through a farm gate and turn right down the concrete track. {J} At the junction with the minor road turn left to walk nearly ¾ mile back into Hartington.

WALK 7
Weage's Bridge, Near Wetton

Weage's Bridge Car Park, Beeston Tor Farm, Throwley Hall Farm, Slade House, Soles Hollow, Manifold Way.

Map: Explorer OL 24
Parking: Grid Ref SK 100 543
Distance: 5½ miles
Approx Time: 3 hours
Grade: 2★
Paths: Trail, field and valley paths.
Stiles: S
Picnic: Instruction 8 is a possibility.

Directions

See directions for walk 7 in the book
Grid Ref SK100543

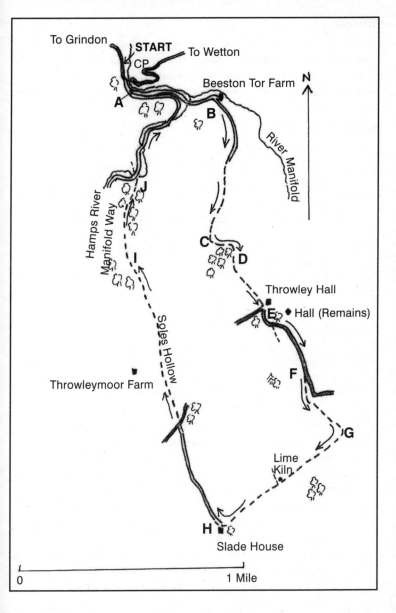

To Grindon
START
To Wetton
CP
Beeston Tor Farm
N
A
B
River Manifold
Hamps River
Manifold Way
J
I
C
D
Throwley Hall
Hall (Remains)
E
Soles Hollow
Throwleymoor Farm
F
G
Lime Kiln
H
Slade House

0   1 Mile

Description

A very stimulating walk in dry sunny weather. The route takes you along tracks and paths across the hills between the Hamps and the Manifold Rivers. The climb to Throwley Hall is gradual but the descent down the lower part of Soles Hollow is fairly steep and can be muddy and slippery after heavy rain. The refreshment stops are mentioned in walk 8.

Route Instructions

1. From the car park walk back to the road. Do not cross the bridge but take the left-hand track. {A} Follow this track, which runs parallel to the cycle route for part of the way, before passing through the caravan site. Continue on down the track towards Beeston Tor Farm.

2. {B} At the farm entrance bear up right on the Throwley Hall and Ilam route. Walk up the track, which eventually becomes a grass track, for about ½mile. You will cross a stile by a gate, pass a barn on the left, and then go through a small gate. As you near the top of the hill the route swings round to the left where you will have a wall on your right for a few metres.

3. {C} At a footpath post turn left away from the wall to walk up to the wood and a waymarked post. Keep the wall and wood close on the right as you follow them round a right hand bend.

4. {D} Go through a small gate to follow a farm track down towards Throwley Hall for a few metres before bearing off right to pass the hall on your left. Go through a small gate in the left hand field corner after passing a silage compound on the left.

5. Follow a path through a small copse to go through a gated stile. Walk through the farmyard towards the hall then follow the Ilam route.

6. {E} Pass the hall on the left to continue along the unfenced road for about ¼mile. {F} At the footpath sign bear right to follow a farm track parallel to the road for a few metres before bearing right up round the hillside. Soon the track bends round left still uphill and with a broken wall on the left. Cross a ladder stile near the top of the hill.

7. The wall is now on the right for a few metres. Just past a gate/gateway cross the wall stile. {G} Keep straight on up the next field aiming for a small gate and with a copse over to the left. [Please note that the wall marked on the OS "White Peak" 1:25,000 map is no longer in evidence]

8. Go through the small gate. Now follow walls close on the left crossing three fields and stiles and passing an old lime kiln.

9. At Slade House turn right along a short walled path to pass the house on your left.

Join a track where you turn right to follow the Soles Hollow route. {H}

10. Stay on this well defined track crossing cattle grids until you reach and cross a minor road.

11. Keep straight on passing a compound [dew pond] and Throwley Moor Farm up on the left. Soon you will have a wall on the left. Pass through two gates and after the second gate the wall is on the right.

12. Continue down the dale. {I} At a sign board keep straight on following the "Soles Hollow" route. This section of the route is in a narrow steep sided valley and could be slippery and muddy after rain. After about 1/2 mile you will reach the Manifold Way via a small gate.

13. {J} Turn right for just over 3/4 mile back to the car park.

WALK 8

Wetton

Wetton, Back of Ecton, Ecton Hill, Wetton Mill, Manifold Way, Wetton.

Map: Explorer OL 24
Start: Grid Ref. SK 109 552
Distance: 5 ½ miles
Approx Time: 3 hours
Grade: 3★
Paths: Moorland, woodland and field paths and trail
Stiles: SSS
Refreshments: Tea Room at Wetton Mill [Not always open in the winter]. The Royal Oak, Wetton.
Picnic: Between F and G may be a possibility.

Directions

From Ashbourne take the A515 Buxton road. In about 5 ½ miles turn left signed Alstonefield. Stay on this road into and through Alstonefield then follow the Wetton signs first down into Hope, where you turn right, still following the Wetton route. The

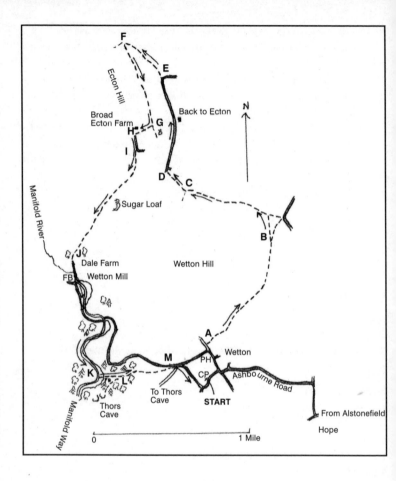

road is very narrow and twisty. On reaching Wetton turn left at the car park and toilet sign. Parking Grid Ref. SK 109552

Description

This is the most challenging walk in the book with the total height climbed 1045ft. It is worth the effort for the wide open views from Ecton Hill across to Hartington and the hills along the Dove to the north east and west to the Manifold Valley. It is an interesting and varied walk following hill and dale paths. Some stretches can be very muddy where animals have churned up the grass. The Tea Rooms and toilets at Wetton Mill make a welcome break but they are not always open in the winter. The Royal Oak in Wetton, [closed at the beginning of the week] the Watts Russell in Hope and The George in Alstonefield all provide refreshment stops.

Route Instructions

1. From the car park turn left down the road and then left again at the T-junction. Walk up through the village ignoring roads off to the right and passing the Royal Oak. Where the road bends left branch off to the right up a wide surfaced lane. Just after passing the "Back of Ecton 1 ½" sign cross the stile on the right. {A}

2. Follow the wall on the right crossing two fields and stiles. The second stile is on right before the field corner. Bear left across the narrow third field. Following the wall on the left across the field and a small copse to go through a stile.

3. Continue ahead in the same north-easterly direction crossing six fields and six stiles. After the gated stile bear left up the seventh field to cross a wall stile by the footpath post.

4. Turn right to follow the wall on the right. At the wall corner keep straight on towards a wall and The National Trust sign over to the right. {B} Just before this sign bear round to the left aiming for a large wall gap by the telegraph pole.

5. Continue ahead with a wall down on the right. As you walk below Wetton Hill, where there are many sheep tracks, you will see a line of widely spaced buildings below the ridge of Ecton Hill. Aim for the house with two dormer windows, below an out crop of rock which is behind it. You will gradually descend into a wide shallow valley.

6. Cross the concrete slabs and bear right to cross a bridge then walk up to and over the stile. {C} Bear right up the field; the house with the dormer windows is now over to your left.

7. Go through a small gate and turn right through the trees to go through another small gate onto the road. {D}

8. Turn right to follow the minor road for about ½ mile and where the road bends down right turn left up a track passing through a small gate by the farm gate. {E}

9. At the top of this ¼ mile track, where it is very muddy, pass the gate across the track to go through a small gate on your left. {F}

10. Follow the top way-marked arrow keeping a fence close on your left. Walk up onto Ecton Hill. Pass through a gated stile and continue across the hillside as indicated by the yellow arrow. Soon you will have an old wall on the left. Cross a squeeze stile and walk towards the wall over on the right.

11. Cross the stile in the field corner by the old copper mining {G] area and immediately turn right over another stile. With the wall close on the left walk down the field, cross the stile by Broad Ecton Farm. Ignore the stile on the left and go through the wall gap in the field corner.

12. {H} Turn left along the farm track and in about 150 metres, where the track turns up left, go through a small gate.{I}

13. Follow the wall on the right down into the valley. Cross a stile by a gate, then a little further on, where the wall turns up right, go through the large wall gap on the right. You now have an old wall then a fence on the left. In the field corner cross the stile onto The National Trust Dale Farm area. In a few metres cross the stile on your left.

14. Walk down the steep partly rocky valley [take care as limestone rocks can be very slippery when wet]. The valley floor soon widens and flattens out.

15. At Dale Farm cross the stile to walk through the farm yard{J} then on down a track to Wetton Mill Tea Rooms and toilets.

16. Cross the bridge over the Manifold river and turn left signed "Wetton 1½ Alstonefield 3". After about ¼ mile along the Manifold Way you have a choice of routes: [a] turn left to follow a winding steep narrow road back into Wetton; or [b] keep straight on over the bridge. The latter is a steeper route up through the woods near Thor's Cave.

17. [b] After crossing the bridge continue along the Manifold Way for a further ¼ mile. Turn left along a clear shale path by the information plaque.{K} Cross the bridge to follow a wide partly stepped and slabbed path up through the trees. [The path to Thor's Cave is off to the right{L}]. Keep straight on up through the woods. Go through a small gate to leave the woods and continue up the valley. As you near the top of the valley cross a stile by a gate.

18. Keep straight on aiming for the road signs and the houses in Wetton village.{M} Cross the stile by the footpath post and turn right along the road.

19. Follow the car parking and toilet signs back to the car park.

WALK 9

Bakewell and Ashford-in-the-Water

Bakewell Station and Monsal Trail Car Park, Churchdale Hall, A6020, Ashford, Wye River Bakewell.

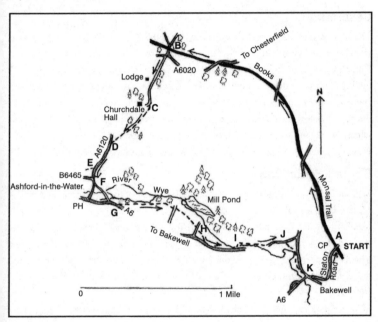

Map: Explorer OL 24
Parking: Grid Ref. SK 223 690
Distance: 5 miles
Approx Time: 2 ¼ hours
Grade: 1
Paths: Trail, drives and riverside paths.
Stiles: S
Refreshments: Bakewell and Ashford.
Picnic: Between {G} and {H}
Wheel Chair: Parts of the Monsal Trail

Directions

From the centre of Bakewell take the A619. After crossing the river bridge turn right immediately then bear left to follow Station Road. At the top of the hill turn right into the car park [pay and display].
Grid Ref SK223690.

Description

The start of the walk from the car park to the A6020 {B} [1 ¾ miles] on the map is wheel chair and pushchair friendly. Once you leave the Trail the route takes you round Churchdale Hall and through the estate to the A6020 then on down a short stretch of the Road to Ashford. Here you can make a detour into the pretty village of Ashford famous for the ancient Sheep Wash Bridge and the well dressings on Trinity Sunday. In the church you will see the relics of another ancient custom, the funeral garlands used when a young girl was buried. There are a number of refreshment stops in the village. Leaving Ashford you will return to Bakewell along the valley of the River Wye.

Route Instructions

1. From the pay and display machine walk past the end of the station buildings to the Monsal Trail. Turn left along the trail. {A}

2. Follow the trail for about 1 ¾ miles in all. You will pass under three bridges, a picnic site and another car park, the back of the County Book Shop at Station Farm, cross a bridleway and lastly cross over the A6020. After passing under the third bridge and just before the second crossing of a road you will leave the trail via a path on the right. {B}

3. At the road junction turn left to walk under the bridge. Cross the A6020, Baslow Ashford road.

4. Walk up the drive signed "Public Footpath". Pass Churchdale Lodge and Hall. By the Hall entrance cross a stile by a gate. In a few metres leave the drive via a stile on the right. {C}

5. Keep straight on down the field passing the Hall on your right. Cross the wall stile near the gateway.

6. Continue ahead down the next field aiming for a valley in mid-distance and passing a stone barn over to the left. Cross a fence stile and continue on down the hill to cross another stile.

7. Follow the rather steep path down through the trees and through a gate to reach the A6020. {D}

8. Turn left along the road for about 200 metres into Ashford. [If you wish to visit this pretty village turn right at the footpath sign on your right] {E}

9. To continue walking back to Bakewell stay on the A6020 passing the B6465 to Monsal Head and the road into the village. Before you reach the A6 turn left down a minor gated road to cross the River Wye. {F}

10. Turn left along the A6 pavement for a few metres then go through a small gate on the left. {G}

11. Keep straight on following the waymarked posts along the undulating Wye valley path. Cross through two small gates, one stile, and one hedge gap then through a second stile.

12. Walk along a fenced path to cross a town road then along another fenced path opposite to cross a stile. {H}

13. Bear right up the field to the road and turn left along the A6. After about 300 metres turn left across the river to the Riverside Business Park Bakewell. {I}

14. Pass the tearooms and turn right to follow a minor road into Bakewell. In about 250 metres after passing the packhorse bridge on the right go through a small gate by the footpath sign. {J}

15. Follow the path across the field to the river. On reaching two gates go through the right hand one and continue along the riverside path. As you near the bridge bear up left to go through a metal gate onto the main road. {K}

16. Cross the road to the central reservation with the stone lamp post. Keep straight on up Station Road for about ¼ mile back to the car park.

WALK 10

Bakewell

Bakewell, Monsal Trail, River Wye, Bowling Green Farm, Calton Pastures, Golf Course. Bakewell.

Map: Explorer OL 24 White Peak
Parking: Grid Ref. SK 223 690
Distance: 5 miles
Approx Time: 2 ½ hours
Grade: 2★ 300ft to 700ft with one difficult descent

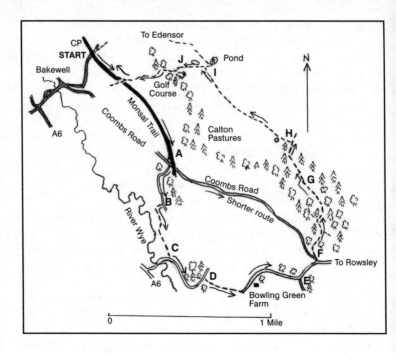

Paths: Trails, tracks and pasture and woodland paths

Stiles: S

Refreshments: In Bakewell

Directions

As for walk 9

Description

The start of the walk along the Monsal Trail to its end [about ¾ mile] is pushchair and wheelchair friendly and although parts of the trail are rather stony the surface is firm. At the end of the trail you can either follow the Coombs Road or take the steeper route along the tracks. The climb up through the beautiful woodland between the Estates of Haddon and Chatsworth will bring you out onto the open expanse of Calton Pastures from which you will have wonderful views over to the Hunting Tower at Chatsworth. Nearing the end of the walk there is a very steep descent down the woodland path to Bakewell golf course; you will need to take great care especially after heavy rain.

Route Instructions

1. From the car park walk past the buildings to the trail and turn right. After about ¾ mile and at the end of the trail turn down right to reach Coombs Road via 12 shallow steps. {A}

2. You can now turn left to follow Coombs Road up to instruction 8 below, or turn left then almost immediately right just before the bridge to follow the left hand track which is the slightly longer and steeper route.

3. Follow the wide track as it circles the hillside. After about 400 metres turn right at the Bridleway sign to go through a small gate then walk down the field keeping a fence close on the right. {B}

4. Turn left at the field corner to follow the field boundary and the river down on your right. Go through the gate ahead and turn left up the minor road. {C}

5. In just over ¼ mile and having gone round a very steep hairpin bend turn right through a small gate on the right to leave the minor road. {D}

6. Follow the "Public Bridleway" up the next three fields, keeping the metal fence close on the right, and going through three gates.

7. Turn left along a track then continue up a wider track passing Bowling Green Farm. At a T-junction of tracks turn left. {E}

8. Walk down the track to join the shorter route. Ignore a gate and track off to the right and keep straight on, leaving the tracks to follow a narrow bridleway up a wooded path. [The shorter route will turn left to follow this bridleway.] {F}

9. After nearly ½ mile up this quite steep path you will join a wider path and turn left. At the Haddon Hall estate notice turn right to continue uphill through the woods.

10. At the top of the hill and reaching a stone gateway and an open viewing area, turn right through the gateway. {G}

11. Follow a path as it swings round to the left through open woodland. This area can be quite wet and muddy because the horses use it. Stay on the wider path passing way marked posts. At a low way marked post near a fence ahead turn right to follow an old wall on the left.

12. Cross a ladder stile to leave the woods and turn left leaving the bridleway. {H} Follow the woodland boundary on the left. At a small fenced area on the left aim for a gate and fence at some distance ahead.

13. Cross a fence stile and keep straight on across Calton Pastures. The path gradually bends round to the right as you aim for another small fenced area ahead.

14. At a gate[do not go through it] turn right following a fence on the left for a few metres then go through a small gate on the left by the pond. {I}

15. Bear left following the Bakewell route. Pass the small fenced copse of trees on your right and continue down the field passing under the power lines. Go through a small gate. {J}

16. Follow the very steep path down through the wood taking great care and ignoring all side paths. Leave the wood to cross the golf course to enter a fenced path. {K}

17. If you wish to return to the car park before visiting Bakewell turn right over a stile, before you reach a metal gate. Walk down to the Monsal Trail, where you turn right to retrace your outward route back to the car park.

18. If you wish to visit the town continue ahead through the metal gate to cross the bridge and stile.

19. Keep straight on down the field to join a drive and go through a gate. Turn left on down the drive to go through another gate. Turn right along Coombs Road into Bakewell. {L}

20. At the road junctions, turn left into town or turn right up Station Road back to the car park.

WALK 11

Birchover and Stanton Moor

Birchover Car Park, Stanton Moor, Barn Farm, Birchover village.

Map: Explorer OL 24
Parking: Grid Ref SK241 625
Distance: 3 miles
Approx Time: 1 ¼ hours
Grade: 1
Paths: Moorland and village road
Stiles: S
Refreshments: In Birchover
Picnic: Stanton Moor instruction 7 before the stile at {G}

Directions

From Bakewell take the A6 south passing Haddon Hall on the left. Turn right to follow the B5056 that takes a left-hand bend after about ¾ mile. Continue along the B5056 for another 1 ¼ miles. Turn left to follow the winding road uphill into and through

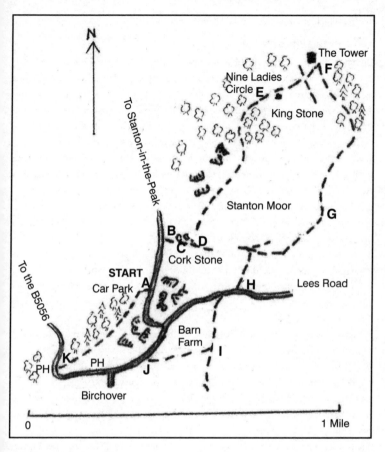

the village. At the top of the hill just past the new quarry workings bear round to the left. The car park is on the left.

Description

An interesting walk for the family where there are historical, archaeological and geological features to investigate. A number of information boards set at points of interest explain the history of the area. There are many side paths as this is an area of open access. Do take care round the old over grown quarry sites. There are two inns in the village "The Red Lion" and "The Druid Inn" named after the Rowter Rocks behind the inn which are thought to have Druid connections.

Route Instructions

1. {A} Leave the car park via the main entrance and turn left up the road.

2. In about 400 metres turn right across the stile by the footpath and Open Access signs. {B} Keep straight on to cross another stile. {C}

3. Follow the Stanton Moor path uphill for 200 metres to The Cork Stone. {D] Turn left and in a few metres, at a fork of paths, bear left through the heather. You will pass the overgrown old quarry areas before entering the open birch woodland.

4. Where you enter a more open area you will see a fence ahead, just before this fence turn right to stay on the main path. This path soon narrows as it crosses the heather. At a fence corner stay on the main path as it bends round to the right. Soon you will pass The King Stone before walking by The Nine Ladies Circle. {E}

5. At the information board cross a wide path to keep straight on. At a fork of paths bear left walking towards the Tower.

6. On reaching the Tower, cross the stile on the left and pass the Tower also on your left. Go down the steps to the "Stanton Moor National Trust" sign. {F}

7. Turn right to follow the path along the top of the escarpment with an old fence close on your right. After about ¾ mile and at the next National Trust sign, turn right over a fence stile. {G}

8. Turn left, ignoring a right hand path, to walk through the heather. At the next crossing of paths turn left down the wider stony path to cross a stile onto the road.

9. {H} Turn right up the road for nearly 100 metres then turn left through the stile.

10. Follow the path down to Barn Farm, first with a fence on the right then a wall and trees on the left. Walk through the farmyard to pass a converted building "Hill Carr Barn" on the right. Keep to the main farm drive, then go through a stile by the gate ahead. {I}

11. Immediately turn right to go across the squeeze stile. [This area can be very muddy] Walk along the edge of the caravan-park to join the farm drive. Walk down to the road.

12. {J} Turn left to walk down through Birchover. In nearly ½ mile, opposite The Druid Inn, turn right up a fairly steep woodland path. {K} Along this path you will see the remains of old stone buildings and quarries. This path ends back at the car park.

WALK 12

Elton

Elton village, Elton Common, Gratton Dale, Dale End, Elton

Map: Explorer OL 24
Parking: Where safe in the village
Start: Grid Ref. SK 222 610
Distance: 4 miles
Approx Time: 2 hours
Grade: 2
Paths: Field and dale paths and minor road.
Stiles: SS
Refreshments: Tea shop in Elton open summer weekends

Directions

From Bakewell take the A6 south towards Rowsley and Matlock. In nearly 2 ½ miles turn right onto the B5056 and in about ¾ mile follow this road round a left-hand

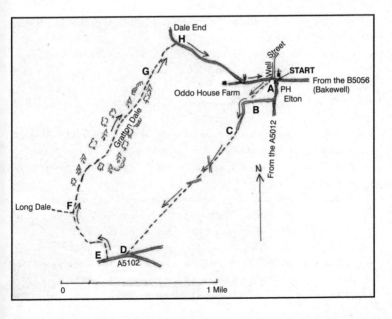

bend crossing the river. Continue along the B5056 for a further 2 ¾ miles when you turn sharp right at the crossroads signed Elton. Drive along the minor road for about ¾ mile into Elton. Park where safe and convenient, as there is no official car park in the village. The walk starts by the church.

Description

For a short walk this is quite varied. Please be aware that this farming area will always be subject to changes. It is advisable to follow this route after a period of dry weather, preferably in the summer, as Gratton Dale can be very muddy. Elton lies on the spring line between the limestone and the gritstone. There are remains of old wells and pumps, notably in Well Street. It was a former lead-mining village with four pubs but only one remains. All Saints Church was rebuilt in 1812 after the collapse of the former building due to mine workings. There is a teashop in the village open during summer weekends.

Route Instructions

1. With the Duke of York pub on your left and the church on your right walk along West End road for a few metres. Just past Well Street and before Elton Village Hall turn left up the path between the houses to cross the stile. {A}

2. Turn right behind the houses and cross the field diagonally to go through a squeeze stile to the left of two gates.

3. Walk round a small copse of fir trees to cross another squeeze stile. Keep straight on across the field ahead to go through another stile. Turn right along a walled track. {B}

4. After about 100 metres turn left up another walled track, at the end of which cross a stile. {C}

5. Walk across the large undulating field following the "Public Footpath to Pikehall" sign and aiming for the power line poles. Pass under the power lines to continue in the same direction. Cross a farm track. There may be a stile to cross depending on the crops grown.

6. Continue in the same direction passing under more power lines, crossing a farm track and then through the stile. Bear slightly right across the next field and through the old low squeeze stile [not a wall gap to the left!]. Cross another farm track.

7. Continue ahead aiming for the road. After crossing the next field and an old stile in a broken wall aim for and pass two stone troughs. Cross the stile ahead and keep straight on crossing three more fields via stiles and a gate.

8. {D} Turn right up the A5012 for about 200 metres. Go through the way marked

farm gate on the right by the Gratton Dale sign. {E}

9. Follow the wall on the left. At the wall corner continue to follow the wall for a few metres before bearing off right downhill to the top of Gratton Dale.

10. Pass through a gateway and further on down the path go through the small gate ahead. {F} [Not the larger gate on the left]

11. Walk down Gratton Dale for nearly 1 ¼ miles in all. About halfway down you will cross a broken wall by the scree slope to follow a wall now on the right. Nearing the end of the dale you will pass through two gates between which you may need to take a higher path to avoid the stream that appears after a period of rain. Notice the old lime-kiln on the left after the second gate. {G}

12. On reaching the road via a stile at Dale End turn right. {H}

13. Walk up Gratton Lane for about ¾ mile back in to Elton Village.

WALK 13

Over Haddon

Over Haddon Car Park, Haddon Fields, Lathkill Dale hill-side, Over Haddon [see book [B]

Map: Explorer OL 24
Parking: Grid Ref SK 203 665
Distance: 3 ½ miles
Approx Time: 1 ½ hours
Grade: 1
Paths: Field paths with good views
Stiles: SS
Refreshments: Lathkill Hotel in Over Haddon

Directions

From Bakewell take the B5055 to Monyash. In a mile bear off left to Over Haddon. Drive into the village and at the junction with School Lane turn right along Main Street to the Pay & Display car park.

Description

A short easy walk across undulating fields east of Over Haddon before walking above the lower reaches of beautiful Lathkill Dale. There are wonderful views towards

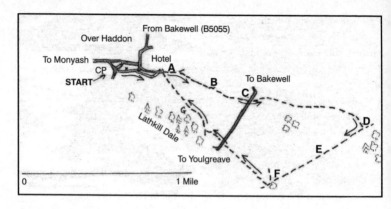

Youlgreave. This is a good picnic area. The only steep slope on this walk is across the two fields back to the village where the Lathkill Hotel and Geoff's Diner provide suitable refreshment stops.

Route Instructions

1. Leave the top part of the car park by the Pay&Display machine to cross the road and walk up Dale Road to join Main Street. Keep straight on passing Geoff's Diner. Bear off right down Wellgate Lane. [Notice the pump and well] Keep straight on past the Lathkill Hotel.

2. {A} Cross the stile ahead and keep straight on up the field to cross a wall and fence stile to the left of a gate.

3. Bear right down the field aiming for two gateways and a wall corner. Cross the stile near the left-hand gateway. {B} Follow the wall close on the left to cross the stile in the field corner and bear slightly left across the next field.

4. {C} Cross the road via two gated stiles then bear left across the field corner to go over a high wall stile. Cross a track and walk on up the field to follow a wall on your left down the large field. Cross the high wall stile near the field corner. You will see a wood over to the right.

5. Bear right down the middle of the next field. Aim for a gate and a fence corner then follow the fence on the right to go through a small gate by the wall ahead. {D}

6. Walk up the next two fields following the wall on the left and crossing the stile a few metres to the right of the first field corner. {E}

7. As you approach the farm walk under the trees go through a small gate or over the wall stile. {F}

8. Bear right across the field following the "Over Haddon" route. From here you will be aiming for the white building of the Lathkill Hotel. Cross three fields, four stiles and a minor road.

9. {G} Walk above the Lathkill River before going through the small gate in the fence on your right. Bear left to start your ascent to the village. Cross two fields and a gated stile under the hawthorn tree before crossing another gated stile onto the road.

10. Walk in front of the hotel then bear right up to the junction where you keep straight on to join Main Street. Keep straight on again to return to the car park.

WALK 14
Lathkill Dale

Youlgreave Moor Lane Car Park, Limestone Way, Cales Dale, Lathkill Dale, Meadow Place Grange, Moor Lane Car Park.

Map: Explorer OL 24
Parking: Grid Ref. SK 194 644
Distance: 5 ½ miles
Approx Time: 2 ½ hours
Grade: 2
Paths: Mainly well used dale paths and field paths.
Stiles: SS
Picnic: In parts of the dale and at {I} on the map.

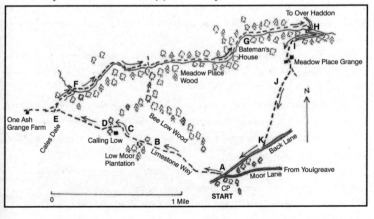

Directions

From Bakewell take the A6 road to Matlock. After passing Haddon Hall car park on the right turn right to follow the B5056 to Youlgreave. Drive through the village to the post office and The Fountain or Conduit Head a 1,500 gallon capacity reservoir built in 1829. Fork right off the main street in the village to follow the narrow Moor Lane uphill for just over a mile. Turn left into Moor Lane pay and display car park.

Description

This is a delightful walk across well-used field paths before descending 171 limestone steps into Cales Dale then along the beautiful Lathkill Dale. You will see the remains of lead mining along the dale. After a period of heavy rain it would be advisable to ring English Heritage on 01629 816640 as parts of the dale can become flooded. For wheelchair users there is a stretch of the dale from the minor road out of Over Haddon to Batemans House, about a 15 minute walk.

Route Instructions

1. Leave the car park via the main entrance and turn left up the road. Cross the road ahead to go through the gated squeeze stile. {A}

2. Keep straight on diagonally across the field. Cross a wall stile and then another gated wall stile over on the right in the next field. Keep straight on up the middle of the large field ahead.

3. Cross the fence stile to continue in the same direction and go through a small gate into Low Moor Wood. Follow the short path through the wood to go through a gate or over the stile. {B}

4. Walk diagonally across the field to the farm. Go through the small gate then another gate on the left. {C}

5. Follow the path through the small open woodland crossing through three gates. Continue down the field, passing barns over to the left, to go through the fourth gate. {D}

6. Bear left down the field to go through a waymarked gate then continue on down the next two fields and through two gates to enter the English Nature area.

7. Follow the 171 limestone steps, which can be slippery when wet, down into Cales Dale. {E}

8. Cross the stile and turn right to follow the narrow path which climbs gently up to join another path. Turn right to continue along the dale.

9. Cross the bridge over the River Lathkill. [This is a pleasant picnic area] {F}

10. Turn right to follow the riverside for two miles in all along Lathkill Dale. You will cross two gates, two stiles and pass a bridge on your right. This bridge leads to the remains of Bateman's house where there is an information plaque. {G}

11. On reaching the minor road from Over Haddon via the second gate, turn right to cross the footbridge. {H}

12. Turn left to follow a wide track quite steeply up out of the dale.

13. {I} Pass through a farm gate and turn left across the field to Meadow Place Grange. Go through the farm gate by the two footpath posts then across the large farmyard via a gate and a wall stile.

14. Walk up the short muddy track, then follow a wall close on the right ignoring the footpath to Youlgreave. When you reach the second footpath sign to Middleton turn left up the field aiming for a short post. {J} Cross the wall stile ahead.

15. Bear slightly left to cross the middle of the next two fields and crossing two stiles.

16. {K} Turn right up the road for nearly ½ mile before turning left to the car park.

WALK 15
Baslow

Baslow Nether End Car Park, Yeld Wood, Gardom's Edge, A619, Dobb Edge, Chatsworth, Baslow.

Map: Explorer OL 24
Parking: Grid Ref SK 258 721
Distance: 6 miles
Approx Time: 3 hours
Grade: 2
Paths: Estate drives, woodland moorland and edge paths.
Stiles: S
Refreshments: Chatsworth and Baslow
Picnic: Instruction 8
Wheel Chair: Chatsworth Park

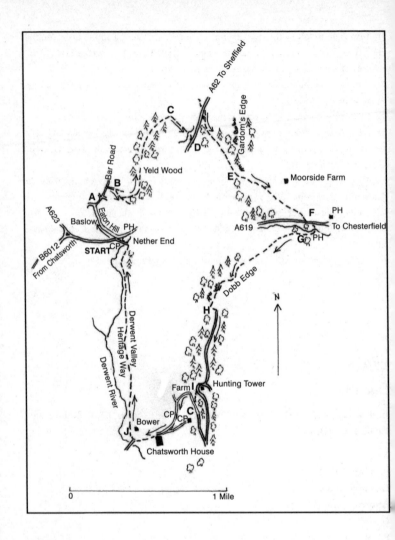

Directions

From the island on the outskirts of Baslow, where the A619 and the A623 meet turn right to Nether End Baslow. After passing The Cavendish Hotel and before the pedestrian lights, fork off right to the pay and display car park on your right.

Description

No Peak District walk book would be complete without a walk in the Chatsworth area. The route starts with a gentle climb up through Baslow before you follow a woodland path through Yeld Wood, a delightful area in the spring, although it can be very muddy in places. The scenery changes to moorland once you have climbed the boulder-strewn path to Gardom's Edge, where the views are worth the climb. This is a good picnic area. The route now winds down across bracken and grass slopes to the A619. You follow the concessionary path across Dobb Edge to the Hunting Tower and on down the 145 steps to Chatsworth House and then along the well used path back to Baslow. You do have the option of starting the walk at the car park by the house between Easter and mid-December. There are a number of refreshment stops in Baslow as well as the restaurant at Chatsworth.

Route Instructions

1. From the car park cross the minor road and The Green to cross the A619 at the pedestrian lights. Walk up Eaton Hill.

2. {A} At the top of the hill turn right up Bar Road. After about 300 metres and having passed Hydro Close on the right turn right, opposite Bar House, along a partly surfaced track passing Moor Cottage on the left. {B}

3. Pass through a small waymarked gate and take the lower path at the edge of the wood. After about 100 metres bear off up to the left through the wood.

4. Follow the woodland path up through Yeld Wood for nearly one mile. [About 20 minutes] At the end of the wood go through a small gate and turn right. {C}

5. Walk down the field to cross a footbridge then on up a track to cross a wall stile by a farm gate onto the A621. {D}

6. Turn left along the pavement for 300 metres and immediately after passing Cupola Cottage on the right cross the busy road to go over a small wall stile by a water trough.

7. Follow the path uphill crossing a stile then walk behind the cottage. At a fence corner turn left to follow the path up towards Gardom's Edge. You will pass through three wall gaps.

8. {E} After the third gap, at the top of the climb, keep straight on. [This is a good picnic place] There are a number of paths in this open bracken and grass area, aim to keep straight on with a wood down on the right. Shortly you will see Moorside Farm over to your left. You should now be walking towards the main road. Pass a farm gate on the left to reach the stile in the wall corner. {F}

9. Cross the stile and turn left along the road for about 50 metres. [If you wish to visit The Robin Hood for refreshment continue along the road for a further 200 metres]

10. Cross the very busy A619 to cross a small stile by one of the Chatsworth signs. Follow the path and steps downhill to cross the footbridge then on up the bank to cross a track and continue up the slope to cross a small ladder stile. {G}

11. Turn left to follow the well-used undulating path across Dobb Edge. You will cross three stiles before following a path across open grassland. Cross a high wall stile and walk up a wide grass path to follow a wall close on your left.

12. {H} Cross another high wall stile and turn left. In a few metres turn right along a track which soon joins a surfaced track. Continue ahead along the estate road for nearly ½ mile and at the T-junction turn right. In a few metres turn right off the estate road below the Hunting Tower. {I}

13. Walk down the 145 steps then across the stream and a path to reach the estate road. Turn right. [If you wish to avoid the steps continue along the estate road passing the waterfall and on reaching a wide T-junction turn right, this will then lead down to Chatsworth House]

14. Follow the estate road past the Farmyard and on down the main drive through the car park, passing close to the House entrance. Follow a narrower path by a fence on the left. [Notice Queen Mary's Bower over to the right] Go through a gate and on up towards the bridge. Just before the bridge turn right then through a gate. {J}

15. Follow the shale path through the park for about one mile. Near the end of the path take a right fork up the unsurfaced path.

16. Pass through a tall black circular gate. Now follow the path back to Baslow and the car park crossing the bridge over Bar Brook.

WALK 16

Calver

Calver village, Calver Peak, Deep Rake, Coombs Dale, A623, Calver.

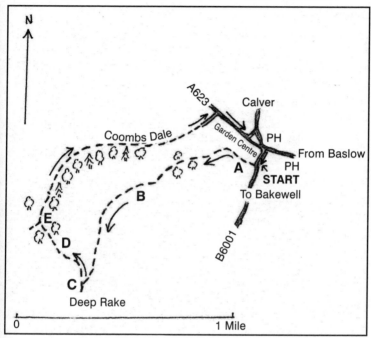

Map: Explorer OL 24
Parking: Where safe in the village
Start: Grid Ref SK 238 747
Distance: 3 ½ miles
Approx Time: 1 ¾ hours
Grade: 2
Paths: Moorland and dale paths and tracks
Stiles: S
Refreshments: In Calver village
Picnic: Between {B} and {C} is a possibility

Directions

From Baslow take the A623 north [Stockport]. After nearly 2 miles park where safe in Calver as there is no official car park. The walk starts at the garden centre entrance off the Bakewell road in Calver.

Description

This is a walk of contrasts. You climb steadily up to Deep Rake quarrying area following clear paths up the valley then across open moorland before the easy descent into Coombs Dale to return along a partly surfaced track back to Calver. There are refreshment stops in Calver and near by Baslow.

Route Instructions

1. Pass the entrance to the garden centre on you right and almost immediately turn right over a stile by the gate to walk up a private drive. Cross another stile by a gate. {A}

2. Continue ahead up the path, and soon you will have a wall on the right as you climb the hill. Go through a gate.

3. Keep straight on gradually climbing the tree lined sunken path. Near the top of the path go through two small gates, crossing a field, to pass the gorse bushes. The distance from the road to this point is about ¾ mile and you will have done nearly all the climb. {B}

4. Follow a fence then a wall on the left and just before a waymarked stile by a gate turn right. {C}

5. Walk downhill towards the telegraph poles, which you pass on your right, then on down the valley to a waymarked post. Continue on a downward path with the wall on the left. {D}

6. Eventually you cross a fence stile on the left and turn right on down the dale. Cross a large wooden stile and walk to the track ahead crossing a small stream. {E}

7. Turn right along the wide partly surfaced track of Coombs Dale. In about ¾ mile you will go round a gate to walk to the A623. {F}

8. Turn right to walk back into Calver.

WALK 17

Eyam

Eyam Car Park, Furness Quarry, A623, Tideswell Lane, Eyam.

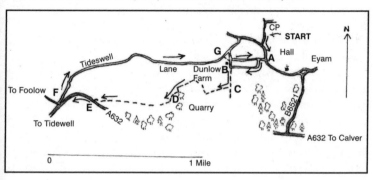

Map: Explorer OL 24
Parking: Grid Ref. SK 216 767
Distance: 3 ½ miles
Approx Time: 1 ½ hours
Grade: 1★
Paths: Minor road, tracks and field paths
Stiles: S
Refreshments: In Eyam
Picnic: Between {D} and {E}

Directions

From Baslow take the A623 north, to drive through Calver and Stoney Middleton. After just over 3 ½ miles turn right to Eyam. As you enter the village bear off left near the top of the hill, then follow the road round to the left. Drive through the village passing the church, hall and post office. Turn right up Hawkhill Road to the car park.

Description

Eyam will repay a visit for it is known as the Plague Village and there are many references to it on the walls of the cottages. The walk is short and undulating with no steep climbs. There is one very short stretch of about 350 metres along the A623 where there is no pavement and the lorries do come round the hill quite fast, so please take care.

ROUTE INSTRUCTIONS

1. Leave the pay and display car park to turn left back down the road then left again. Opposite Eyam Hall craft area turn right down New Close. {A}

2. Pass the entrance to Eyam Hall car park to turn left up the narrow Dunlow Lane. Follow the lane round to the right. Walk up the hill with houses on the right to Dunlow Farm entrance. {B}

3. Turn left to follow the walled track and just before stone gate posts turn right along a grass walled track signed Housley. {C}

4. Go through a small waymarked gate and keep straight on crossing three fields. After going through another small gate turn right up round the old quarry. Pass a footpath post to keep straight on then go through another gate. Now follow a broken wall on the right and the quarry fence on the left. [In the summer this path could be overgrown and you may need to walk in the field on the right]

5. Ignore a stile on the left. Cross a ladder stile, turn left then right to follow the wall on the right as you descend the hillside on the line of an old track. Cross the stile by the farm gate and keep straight on up the scrubland. [Maybe somewhat overgrown] {D} Cross a large planked stile by a gate.

6. Continue up the hill with broken walls up on the right and down on the left. [A possible picnic area] Eventually you will descend to the very busy A623 where you have to cross the stile onto the road and turn right. Take great care! {E}

7. After about 350 metres turn right signed Foolow and Housley then immediately turn right again to follow Tideswell Lane. [Unsuitable for Motors] {F}

8. Follow this undulating twisting track for just over a mile. When you reach the houses and surfaced lane turn right to walk across the field. {G} Go through two wall gaps then on down the surfaced path to join the road.

9. Keep straight on to turn left along the main street in the village back to Hawkhill Road and the car park.

WALK 18
Shillito Wood

Shillito Wood Car Park, Ramsley Reservoir, A621, Bar Brook, Car Road, Hewetts Bank, Shillito Wood.

Map: Explorer OL 24
Parking: Grid Ref. SK 295 750
Distance: 5 miles
Approx Time: 2 ¼ hours
Grade: 1
Paths: Moorland and woodland paths
Stiles: S
Picnic: Instruction 4

Directions

From Baslow take the A619 Chesterfield road; at the roundabout just beyond Baslow take the A621 Sheffield road. In just over 1 ½ miles and shortly after crossing a cross roads bear off right at the parking sign. Follow the minor road for another 1 mile. Ignore a right turn and drive up another 250 metres to turn right into the small car park. Grid Ref. SK 295750

Description

An easy walk at any time of the year. The route is along well-defined moorland paths. There are only three stiles and one short climb back to the car park. The car park would be a suitable picnic spot although there are no tables.

There are a number of refreshment places in Baslow.

Route Instructions

1. Leave the car park via the main entrance and turn left down the road passing a road on the left. In about ½ mile turn right over a stile by a gate.{A}

2. Before you reach the two gates ahead, bear off left to follow a path down through the trees with the fence and embankment over to the right. At the fence corner bear up right to a wider moor land path.

3. Follow the wide moorland path, which shortly bends round to the right, for nearly ½ mile. Cross the stile onto the A621.{B} Turn right for a few metres then cross the road to go over a stile by a gate onto the Eastern Moors estate.

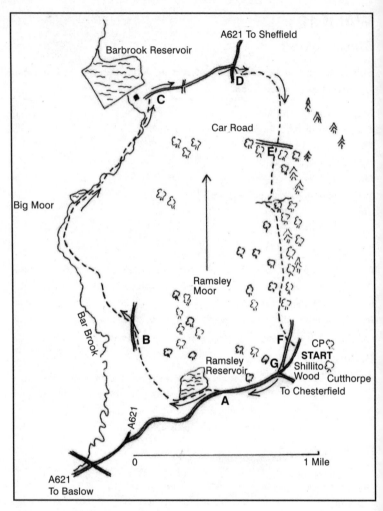

4. Continue ahead along the moorland path. Soon you will be following the line of Bar Brook. In about 1 ¼ miles and just after passing the water works buildings turn right at the T-junction of tracks.{C}

5. In nearly ½ mile go through the gate and cross the busy A621 to cross a stile by a gate.{D}

6. Follow a wide, partly shale covered track down through the scrub land for about ¾ mile. Cross a stile by a gate then cross a rocky track [Car Road], to go through the small gate.{E}

7. Follow the fence on the left up a wide grass track which winds gradually up the valley for about 1 mile.

8. As the track flattens you will possibly see cars on the road ahead. Look to the left where you will see a gate onto the road by the car park.{F} Turn left up a narrow grass path, cross another track, then pass through the gate and stile to cross the road back to the car park.

[Should you miss this path back to the car park the track will take you to the road {G} where you turn left to walk up the road back to the car park.]

WALK 19

Chelmorton

Chelmorton, Town Head Farm, Taddington, Chelmorton.

Map: Explorer OL 24
Parking: Where safe and convenient in the village.
Start: Grid Ref. SK 115 703
Distance: 4 ½ miles
Approx Time: 2 ¼ hours
Grade: 3
Paths: Field paths, tracks and minor roads
Stiles: SSS
Refreshments: Chelmorton.
Picnic: Instruction 11 is a possibility

Directions

From Buxton take the A515 Ashbourne road and in nearly 3 ½ miles turn left onto the A5270 and in nearly 1 mile turn right then left both signed Chelmorton. Park where safe in the village. The walk starts at the church.

Description

A pleasant walk with far reaching views across the farmland and tracks between Chelmorton, the highest village in Derbyshire, and Taddington. The Church Inn at the start

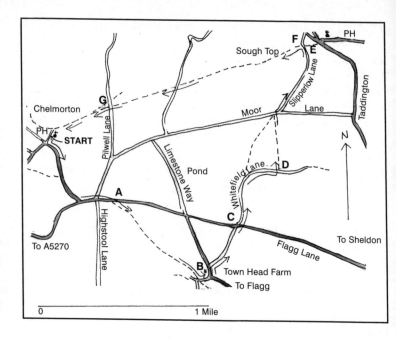

of the walk and The Queens Arms in Taddington are suitable refreshment stops; an extra mile would be added onto the walk to reach The Queens Arms.

Route Instructions

1. With the church on the left walk down the road to take the first turn left. Follow the road up hill for about ¼ mile to turn left at the T-junction. In 300 metres, and having kept straight on at a crossroads, turn right at the footpath post.{A}

2. Bear left across the field aiming to the left of a field corner then bear off left down the field to follow a wall on the left. Cross the stile in the field corner.

3. Bear slightly left up the next three fields crossing three stiles, in the third field aim for the bottom right hand corner of a wood. In the fourth field turn right passing Town Head Farm on your left. Cross the stile by a gate then another stile ahead to reach the road. [a very muddy area and you may need to reach the road via a gate down on the left] {B}

4. Turn left along the road and at the T-junction turn left signed Chelmorton. In about 100 metres turn right up a wide walled partly surfaced track.

58

5. Cross the Chelmorton to Sheldon road to follow Whitefield Lane.{C} About 400 metres after a right hand bend turn left across a fence stile.{D}

6. Walk up the next two fields following the broken wall on the right and crossing the stile in the field corner.

7. Turn right along Moor Lane for 75 metres then left to follow Slipperlow Lane to the outskirts of Taddington; nearly ½ mile.{E}

8. Just before you reach the first buildings turn left at the "Public Footpath to Chelmorton 2"sign.{F}

9. Follow the steep path uphill crossing three fields and a stile in the corner of the third field. Continue in the same direction towards the masts and Sough Top. Cross the stile in the field corner.

10. Keep straight on to cross another stile by a gateway. Now follow field boundaries on your right to cross nine fields and stiles and a track. After the tenth field, where there is no wall on the right, cross the stile and turn right up Pillwell Lane and almost immediately turn left through a small gate.{G}

11. Keep straight on across the undulating old lead mining area before descending on a wide grassy track back to Chelmorton.

WALK 20
Errwood Reservoir

Errwood Reservoir Car Park, The Street, Pym Chair, The Tors, Shining Tor, Stake Side, Errwood Reservoir.

Map: Explorer OL 24
Parking: Grid Ref SK 013 757
Distance: 6 miles
Approx Time: 3 hours
Grade: 3
Paths: Minor road and moorland paths.
Stiles: S
Picnic: At {C} and between {F} and {A}

Directions

From Buxton take the A5004 Whaley Bridge road and in about 2 ¼ miles turn left to the Goyt Valley. Follow the minor road for 1 ½ miles and just after crossing the

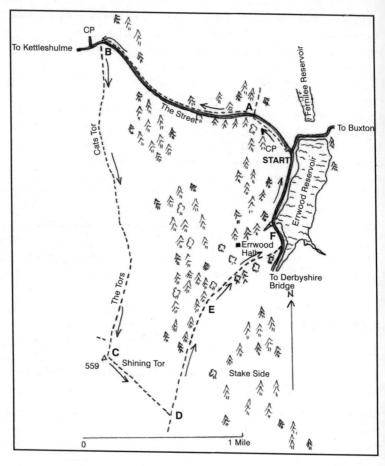

reservoir turn right into the car park.

Description

This is a walk of scenic grandeur which repays the effort of the initial climb up the well–defined path to Pym Chair. You will be following clear paths across open moorland between 400 and 500 metres [1,450ft] so it is advisable to take wind proof clothing and choose a clear day. On the very easy return route by the reservoir there are a number of picnic spots.

Route Instructions

1. Walk through the car park then along a path parallel to the Kettleshulme road for just under ¼ mile. Cross the road level with double farm gates and the Midshires Way route to turn left and follow the path with the road now on your left.{A}

2. In 1 ½ miles from the car park and at the top of the hill before the Pym Chair car park leave the road to turn left up the bank to cross the fence stile onto the Access Land.{B}

3. Follow the Shining Tor route across The Tors for 2 miles keeping a broken wall on the right. You will cross two broken walls and parts of the middle stretch may be quite muddy. As you near Shining Tor ignore a footpath off to the right.

4. On reaching the Trig. Point at Shining Tor turn left signed "Cat & Fiddle and Stake Side".{C}

5. Follow the clear path down then up to go through a small gate. Turn left to follow a wall close on the left.{D}

6. After just over ¾ mile, and having passed between two old gateway posts, bear off right signed "Errwood Reservoir and car parks"{E}

7. Walk down the wide grass path through a gate and on down aiming for a gateway to the right of a wood.

8. Pass through the gateway to follow the path back to the reservoir.{F} Turn left by the car park to walk along the reservoir road back to your car park; about ¾ mile.

WALK 21

Peak Forest

Peak Forest, Old Dam Lane, The Cop, Limestone Way, Sweetknoll Farm, Eldon Lane Old Dam.

Map: Explorer OL 24 White Peak and OL 1 Dark Peak
Parking: Where safe and convenient in Peak Forest.
Start: Grid Ref. SK 115 792
Distance: 4 miles
Approx Time: 2 hours
Grade: 2

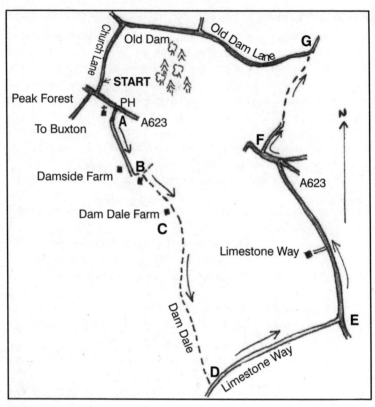

Paths: Minor road and moorland paths

Stiles: S

Refreshments: In Peak Forest

Picnic: {D} on the map is a possibility

Directions

and parking the same as for walk 22

Description

This walk across open moorland takes you on a route north of the previous walk. These two walks could easily be joined, leaving out Old Dam Lane, as you can see from the map. This would give you a walk of 6 ½ miles grade 2. Follow Walk 23 first then when you reach Old Dam Lane continue ahead to follow this walk route.

Route Instructions

1. Start at the Post Office and General Store in Church Lane. Walk along the road away from the A623 to the junction with Old Dam Lane. {A} Turn right up the lane for ¾ mile then round a left hand bend{B} on up to The Cop.

2. {C} At The Cop go through a small gate on the right and bear left up the field to go through another small gate. Now keep straight on up the steep rutted walled track and through a third small gate. {D}

3. Now follow a wall close on the left gradually descending the moorland. You will pass through a gate then by a dewpond before crossing a small fence stile.

4. {E} Bear right to a broken wall then follow a wall again close on the left.

5. After 1 ¼ miles from The Cop you will pass through a gate and turn left to go over a stile, changing your direction and leaving the Limestone Way. {F}

6. Follow the wide walled track to cross a stile by a gate where the track turns right.

7. Now keep straight on with a wall close on the left following a stony farm track and crossing two stiles. At the second stile ignore a path off to the left {G} and continue along the track to the bridleway sign. {H}

8. Turn left to walk down to and through a small gate then along a short fenced path to go through another small gate.

9. In a few metres bear off up right to the post ahead; now continue across the hillside walking parallel to the wall down on the left. As you get nearer the wall ignore the stile over to your left and continue round a right hand bend through the hummocky grassland still with the wall on the left.

10. As you descend the field cross a stile by a gate and continue down the field; keep the wall on your left. As you near Sweetknoll Farm bear right away from the wall to go over the stile by the gate. {I}

11. Walk down the stony track to pass the farm and on down the drive, Eldon Lane, to the road where you turn left back to Old Dam. {J} Turn right along Church Lane back to the car.

WALK 22

Peak Forest

Peak Forest, A623, Damside Farm, Dam Dale, Limestone Way, Old Dam Lane, Peak Forest

Map: Explorer OL 24
Parking: Where safe and convenient in Peak Forest
Start: SK 114 794
Distance: 4 miles
Approx Time: 1 ¾ hours
Grade: 1
Paths: Dale paths and tracks
Stiles: S
Refreshments: Peak Forest
Picnic: Between {F} and {G}

Directions

From Buxton take the A6 north and in 2 miles, having driven through the golf course, turn right to Peak Dale. Follow this road for nearly 3 miles passing through the quarrying villages of Peak Dale and Small Dale. At a T-junction with the road to Wormhill stay on the major road round to the left and drive up to the A623 where there are traffic lights. Turn right then immediately left into Church Lane. Park where safe and convenient. The walk starts at the Devonshire Arms on the main road.

Description

In contrast to many of the Peak District dales Dam Dale is much quieter and more peaceful whilst being easy to follow. The only climb comes at the end of Dam Dale when you will follow the Limestone Way to Old Dam Lane This lane is a pleasant stroll back to the car.

Route Instructions

1. From the Devonshire Arms cross the road to walk down Damside Lane passing the church [at one time known as the Gretna Green of the Peak]. {A}
2. Walk through Damside Farm to cross a stile by a gate. At the footpath post turn left to follow a fence on the left then turn right signed "Dam Dale." {B}
3. Cross a wall stile and walk behind a house. Continue ahead keeping a wall down on

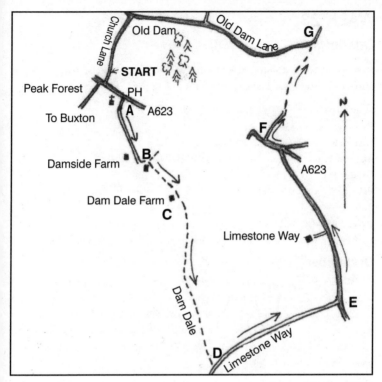

the right before veering away from it, then down towards it again to cross a wall stile. You will now be following the "Public Footpath Miller's Dale" route.

4. Walk behind Dam Dale Farm passing through a gate then following a wall close on the right.{C}

5. Walk down the grassy Dam Dale crossing 4 broken walls and 5 stiles.

6. {D}After the sixth stile turn left up the wide track of the Limestone Way. After about ½ mile at the road junction turn left along the minor road {E} for another ½ mile to the busy A623.

7. Cross the road and turn left. In 100 metres turn right through the waymarked gate {F}. Now follow the wide walled mainly grass track of the Limestone Way for just under ½ mile, going through a gate and across a stile to reach Old Dam Lane. {G}

8. Turn left along the lane to Old Dam for ¾ mile {H}. At the grass island turn left down Church Lane back to the car.

WALK 23

Castleton

Castleton Visitor Centre, Speedwell Cavern, The Winnats, Rowter Farm Limestone Way, Cave Dale, Castleton

Map: Explorer OL 1 Dark Peak
Parking: SK 149 830
Distance: 4 miles
Approx Time: 2 hours or over if the ground is wet.
Grade: 3*
Paths: Tracks and dale paths
Stiles: S
Refreshments: Castleton
Parking: In Castleton park in the pay and display car park at the Visitor Centre.

Description

" A Challenge Walk". The route starts with an easy stroll to the Speedwell Caverns then you ascend the very dramatic Winnats pass; a sight not to be missed. The next section is along easy tracks and paths before you descend into Cave Dale. The lower section of the dale is steep, rocky and could be wet but is very grand and exciting! Here a stick could be helpful. As you reach the bottom the dale opens out to give good views of Peveril Castle.

Route Instructions

1. From the car park return to and cross the main road. Follow the Riverside Walk, a surfaced path, to the minor road where you turn right. Cross the river bridge and walk up Goose Hill and on ahead to join a stony wooded track and go through a gate.{A}

2. Follow a path for ½ mile keeping a wall close on the right until you reach the road at the Speedwell Cavern. {B}

3. Turn left, pass the entrance to the cavern and walk up the Winnats on a path to the right of the road. After about ½ mile ignore a gate on the right and continue ahead up to and through a small gate, still following the road and now with a wall on the left.

4. Just before Winnats Head Farm go through the small gate. Continue up the road crossing the cattle grid. After about 325 metres, at a road junction, keep straight on along the B6061. In 75 metres turn left through a gate way signed "Rowter Farm". {C}

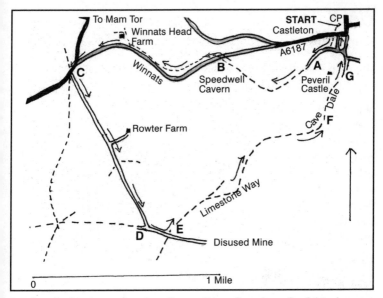

5. Follow the driveway up to and past Rowter Farm where the surfaced drive becomes a stony track. Ignore all paths left and right until you reach another track at the T-junction. [Nearly 1 mile from the B6061]. {D}

6. Turn left for about 250 metres and cross the wall stile by a gate. Immediately turn left onto the Limestone Way {E} going through two gates, then bear right at the Castleton bridleway sign.

7. Walk across the large field aiming for the peak of Lose Hill on the horizon. On reaching a waymarked post follow the blue bridleway sign to go through a small gate. Bear left following the remains of an old wall on the right, to go through another gate. Now keep a wall on the left down the dale. At the next waymarked post continue down a track. Eventually you pass through another gate. So far you have walked about 1 mile from the Castleton sign. {F}.

8. The next ¼ mile is the very steep rocky section that could be flowing with water after heavy rain.

9. As you near the bottom the dale opens out giving good views of Peveril Castle, before a short narrow path which leads into Pindale Road at the top of Castleton. {G}

10. Turn left then right down Castle Street to the main road where you turn left again back to the car park.

WALK 24

Hope

Hope Car Park, Edale Road, Spring House Farm, Losehill Hall, Hollowford Road, Castleton, Peakshole Water, Hope

Map: Explorer OL 1 Dark Peak
Parking: Grid Ref. SK 171 835
Distance: 4 miles
Approx Time: 2 hours
Grade: 1
Paths: Tracks and field paths
Stiles: SS
Refreshments: In Hope and Castleton
Picnic: Instruction 14

Directions

Hope is on the A6187 Hathersage to Castleton road.
Parking in the main "Pay and Display" car park near The Woodruff Arms.

Description

This is an easy walk across open farmland to the north and south of the A6187. There are refreshment places in Hope and Castleton as well as suitable picnic areas along the Peakshole Water route.

Route Instructions

1. From the car park turn right passing the Woodruff Arms then immediately turn left up Edale Road {A} After ¼ mile, and at the "No Through Road" sign down to Killhill Bridge on the right, turn left up steps and through the stile by the footpath sign. {B}

2. Cross another stile to walk up the small paddock keeping the fence close on the left to go through the farm gate. Immediately turn right to follow the Losehill route.

3. Continue in this direction crossing small fields and going through three small gates and over a stile. Follow the path across the railway over a stile then through a small gate. {C}

4. Cross a minor road to walk up the bungalow driveway passing the garages to go through a small gate.

5. Keep straight on along a fenced path to cross a stile, now you will walk up a short

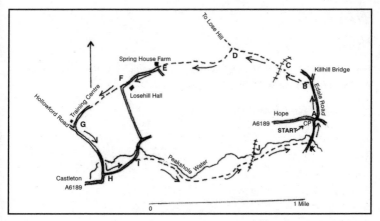

sunken path to go through two gates ahead. Follow the hedge on the left to go through another gate and keep straight on.

6. When you reach a metal footpath sign to Mam Tor {D} turn down left on the Castleton route following the waymarked signs to have a fence on the right. Go through the small gate.

7. Follow the field boundaries on the left crossing three fields, stiles gates and small footbridges, until you have field boundaries on the right for the next three fields. In the third field go through the gate on the right.

8. Follow the path to Spring House Farm {E} where you turn left then right following the Castleton route.

9. Follow the track for about ¼ mile, ignoring a track on the right, to walk behind Losehill Hall. Leave the track where it turns left to go through the small gate ahead. {F}

10. Keep straight on down the field going through the gate and over the stepping-stones. Continue in the same direction before bearing left to follow the track. In about ¼ mile pass the training centre to reach the Hollowford Road. {G}

11. Turn left to walk into Castleton, nearly ½ mile; {H} then turn left along the A 6187 for another ¼ mile. Turn right at the green metal sign for Hope. {I}

12. Walk along the walled track then follow Peakshole Water. Continue in the same direction to cross a stile, a broken wall and then follow a fence on the right.

13. Cross the stile and keep straight on crossing four fields and stiles before crossing the railway line and another stile. {J}

14. Follow the clear path above the river for about ¼ mile to the road. {K}

15. Turn left down Pindale Lane then left at the main road to return to the car park.

WALK 25

Hope

Hope Car Park, Pinfold Lane, Eccles Lane, Brough, Townfield Lane, Shatton, A 6187, Hallum Barn, Killhill Bridge, Hope.

Map: Explorer OL 1 Dark Peak
Parking: Grid Ref. SK 171 835
Distance: 5 miles
Approx Time: 2 ½ hours
Grade: 2
Paths: Minor roads and field paths
Stiles: SSS
Refreshments: In Hope and the Garden Centre on the A6187

Directions

and PARKING. The same as for Walk 25

Description

Like the previous walk this route follows undulating tracks and field paths to the south and north of the River Noe. This is a pleasant walk for a late spring evening. The only steep climb is up from Brough onto Townhill Lane. The only refreshment facility after Hope is the Garden Centre on the A6187.

Route Instructions

1. Leave the car park to pass The Woodroffe Arms then turn right down Pinfold Lane.{A} In 250 metres turn left up Eccles Lane and in another 100 metres turn left by the footpath post and bench to cross the stile.{B}

2. Keep straight on passing through the gate then bearing right up the wide grass path to go through a gateway.

3. Follow a wood and fence close on the right crossing three fields, two stiles and a footbridge. Keep straight on to cross a ladder stile by the description of the Navio Roman Fort. Bear right down to the road in Brough.{C}

4. Turn left along the road for nearly 100 metres then turn right up Brough Lane by the No Through Road sign.{D}

5. In nearly 300 metres where the lane bends round to the right keep straight on up a track. After going through the third gate follow a hedge close on the right to go

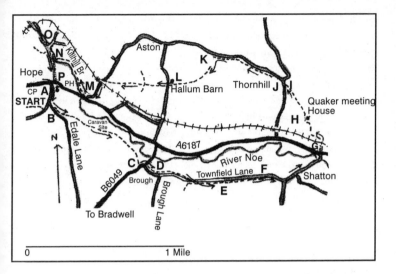

through another gate at the end of the track.

6. {E} Turn left along Townfield Lane for a few metres the along a path parallel to the lane. Soon you will walk behind the barns to go through a small gate then across a stile. Keep straight on to go through another small gate then down steps to continue down Townfield Lane. {F}

7. Cross the ford via a footbridge and continue ahead to walk down through Shatton to the main A6187.

8. Cross the busy road, turn left then almost immediately right to follow the "Thornhill & Yorkshire Bridge" route. {G} Cross the top of the garden centre car park to go under the railway bridge and turn left.

9. Follow the line of the railway and as you near the end of the field turn right away from the railway to follow a hedge close on the left aiming for the big house ahead. Cross the stile by a gate passing the house on the right. [Quaker Meeting House]{H}

10. Immediately turn right along the narrow woodland path to cross a track then through a small gate to follow the Thornhill route This is a very pretty path through an area of spring flowers which leads to the road in Thornhill. {I}

11. Turn right in the village then left up past Nicholas Hall and the chapel. Just opposite Town Head Lane turn left through a stile. {J}

12. Follow the hedge close on the right walking parallel to the road to cross two gates and two stiles. At the signpost "Hope via Hallum Barn" turn left down the field. {K}

13. Cross a footbridge in the right hand field corner. Bear left across the field corner to cross a stile by a gate. Follow the track up to Hallum Barn going through a small gate and a farm gate by the barns.{L}

14. Cross the minor road and the stile. Keep straight on crossing three fields and stiles and a footbridge. In the fourth field bear left down to the railway crossing two stiles.

15. Walk down to the road and turn left under the bridge. Stay on this minor road for 400 metres then turn right along the main road for a few metres to cross a stile on the bridge. Descend the steps to follow the River Noe on your left.{M}

16. Pass through three gates and stiles to reach the mill via a short flight of steps.{N}

17. Turn right up the track to Killhill Bridge.{O} Turn left to the Edale Road then left again to walk back into Hope along the Edale road. At the main road turn right back to the car park.{P}

WALK 26

Ladybower Reservoir

Hurst Clough Car Park, Crookhill Farm, Hagg Side, Ladybower Reservoir.

Map: Explorer OL 1 Dark Peak
Parking: Grid Ref. SK 180 886
Distance: 3 ½ miles
Approx Time: 1 ¾ hours
Grade: 2
Paths: Reservoir road and moorland paths
Stiles: S
Picnic: Between {C} and {E} is a possibility. Reservoir Hurst Clough Car Park, Crookhill Farm, Hagg Side, Reservoir Road.

Directions

From the A625 Hathersage to Castleton road turn right up the A6013 to Bamford. Drive through Bamford to the T-junction with the A57. Turn left crossing the viaduct, then turn right up the minor road along side the reservoir. In just over ¾ mile turn into the Hurst Clough Car Park.

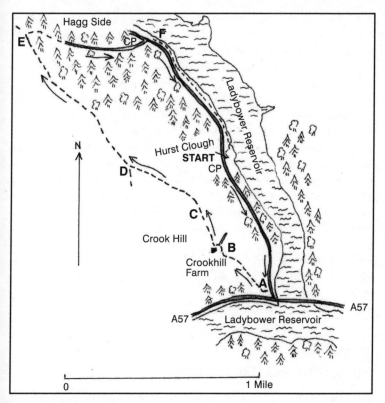

Description

After the initial steady climb of just over ¼ mile up to Crookhill Farm the route across the open moorland and fields is very exhilarating with wonderful views over the reservoir to the Derwent Moors. The return track leads down through the woodland then back along the reservoir road to the car park. There is a path close to the reservoir if you do not wish to use the road.

Route Instructions

1. From the car park turn right back down the road to within about 100 metres before the junction with the A57.{A}

2. Turn right up the bank to go through the small gate. Keep straight on up the field first with a fence on the right then on up the middle of the field to the top right hand

corner. Cross the stile and continue up hill to go through a gate. {B} Turn right to follow the alternative route through another gate then bear left aiming for the right hand end of the barn ahead and the waymarked post.

3. Go through small gates crossing a track and still on the alternative route. Walk up the next field to go through a farm gate in the top right hand corner.

4. {C} Turn right to follow the bridleway route to Rowlee. Go through the gate. Continue on the grass track round Crook Hill following the waymarked posts. As you near a wall over to the left the bridleway bends round to the right.

5. On reaching the wall ahead go through the gate still following the Rowlee Route {D} Keep straight on up the next two fields going through a small gate.

6. As you reach the brow of the hill at 390 metREs [1,279 ft.] aim for the left hand corner of the coniferous wood. Pass through the gate and keep straight on to the follow the wood close on the right for nearly ½ mile passing through a small gate.

7. On reaching a farm gate ahead cross the stile or go through the gate on the right. {E}

8. Walk down the path parallel to a wide stony track. [You may need to use the track in some places] In just over ¾ mile you will join the reservoir road by a car park. {F}

9. Turn right back to Hurst Clough Car Park via the road or the footpath below the road [¾ mile.]

WALK 27

Higger Tor and Carl Wark

Longshaw Estate Car Park, Houndkirk Road, Burbage Rocks, Higger Tor, Carl Wark, Burbage Brook, Longshaw Eastate.

Map: Explorer OL Dark Peak
Parking: Grid Ref. SK 267 801
Distance: 5 miles
Approx Time: 2 ¾ hours
Grade: 2*
Paths: Moorland and edge paths
Stiles: S
Refreshments: The Fox House Inn, Longshaw Visitor Centre, weekends only in the winter. Limited opening in the spring and autumn, open daily June to Sept.
Picnic: Instruction 10

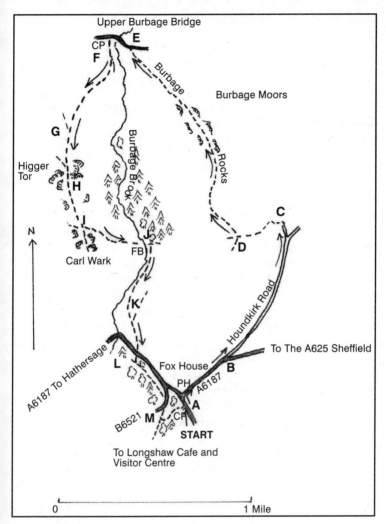

Upper Burbage Bridge

CP E

F

Burbage

Burbage Moors

G

Burbage Rocks

Higger Tor

H

Burbage Brook

N

I

J

Carl Wark

FB

D

C

Houndkirk Road

K

A6187 To Hathersage

L

Fox House

B

To The A625 Sheffield

PH A6187

A

M CP

B6521

START

To Longshaw Cafe and Visitor Centre

0   1 Mile

Directions

From Hathersage take the A6187 Sheffield road. Follow this road for just over 3 miles to The Fox House Inn where you ignore the Sheffield road on the left to continue along the A6187 for a few metres. Turn right into the National Trust car park of The

Longshaw Estate. Grid Ref. SK267801

Description

A very stimulating walk across the open access moorland to the north east of Hathersage, before descending to the pretty Burbage valley at the northern end of Padley Gorge. The short descent down the rocks of Higger Tor could be quite difficult. The Fox House Inn and the visitor centre at The Longshaw Estate are two suitable refreshment stops. The opening times for the visitor centre are:-

1. Weekends–November to March
2. Wednesday to Sunday–March to June and September to November
3. June to September–Everyday.

Route Instructions

1. Return to the main road and turn left towards The Fox House.{A} At the road junction turn right along the Sheffield road. After about ¼ mile bear off left onto a wide stony track. [Houndkirk Road] {B}

2. Follow the track for about ¾ mile. At the gas pipeline signs bear off left, leaving the track, to follow a wide sandy path [big pools after rain!], which shortly bends round to the right before turning left through the heather. Soon you will see another low gas marker over to the right after which you come to a T-junction of paths. {C}

3. Turn left along the peaty path and in about ¼ mile, at a waymarked post, {D} turn right to continue along a rocky moorland path for 1 mile. Keep to the route above the rock outcrops of Burbage Rocks.

4. {E} Cross a fence stile and turn left along the road to cross two bridges. Turn left into the car park to go through a small gate back onto the access land.

5. {F} Take the right hand fork to follow the higher rocky path. As you climb you will soon reach a point where you can see the rocky steps up to Higger Tor. Aim for these steps as you negotiate the rocky path.

6. Climb the steps up to Higger Tor [the steepest part of the walk]. At the top of the climb you come to a T-junction of paths, turn left to pass short wooden posts. {G} Keep straight on to cross the rocky top of Higger Tor; the path winds through and over the flat millstone rocks. Aim to keep over to the left. When you reach the end of the rocks you will see the wide path which leads up to the ancient fort outcrop of Carl Wark.

7. There are a number of places where you can scramble steeply down through the rocks to the Carl Wark path. {H}

8. Join the Carl Wark path and ignore paths off to the left. When you reach the wide path up to the ruins of the old fort turn left below the rock outcrops. {I}

9. Follow the meandering path downhill aiming for the right hand end of a conifer wood.{J}

10. Cross the little stone bridge over Burbage Brook and climb up the bank to the waymarked post. Turn right along the grassy and rocky path to follow the brook down on the right.

11. After nearly ½ mile, at a dew pond, the path starts to veer off left uphill to join a wider path.{K} Turn right along this path to the main road.

12. Cross the road to go through a small gate into the Longshaw Estate.{L]

13. Follow the path which shortly meets another path coming in on the right. Continue ahead walking parallel to the road up on your left. Cross a small gated stile onto the road.

14. Turn right and cross the road to enter the drive leading to the visitor centre and the car park.{M} To return to the car park take the first left turn then another left turn up through the woods.

WALK 28

Tideswell

Tideswell Dale Car Park, B6049, Tideswell Village, Limestone Way, Miller's Dale, Tideswell Dale.

Map: Explorer OL 24
Parking: Grid Ref SK 154 742
Distance: 6 miles
Approx Time: 3 hours
Grade: 1
Paths: Field and dale paths
Stiles: S
Refreshments: In Tideswell and Miller's Dale
Picnic: Tideswell Dale

Directions

From the centre of Tideswell take the B6049 south to Miller's Dale and in a mile turn left into the car park.

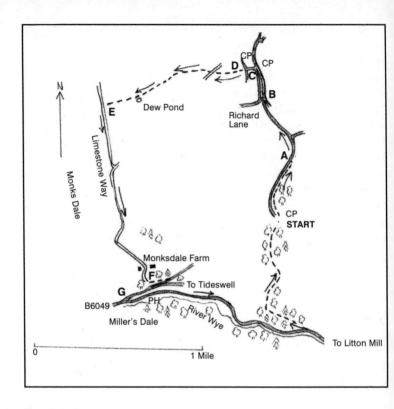

Description

The Cathedral of the Peak, parish church, is well worth a visit. This large village has an interesting history recorded in the Domesday Book. There are a number of books and pamphlets giving the historical background.

The gradual climb up from the car park, through the village and the fields leading to the Limestone Way, is not difficult. The track to Miller's Dale is gently downhill. You then will follow the pretty minor road alongside the River Wye before turning up the peaceful easy path of Tideswell Dale.

Route Instructions

1. From the car park walk up towards the village keeping the road on the left. First you will have a line of beech trees on the left then you pass through a small gate to

follow a wall on the left. When you reach a gate on the left go through it then cross the road to walk up into Tideswell. {A}

2. Just after Richard Lane on the left, on the outskirts of the village, turn left up stone steps by the bus stop. {B} Turn right along the narrow village road, Thorncliffe Terrace and just before The Horse and Jockey turn left up the steep Primrose Lane. {C}

3. Cross the road diagonally right to go through the stile by a gate. {D}

4. Walk up three fields keeping a wall close on the right. Cross a track diagonally to go over the stile. Keep straight on with the wall still on the right to cross four fields. In the fifth field bear left over the stile then continue ahead to cross three more fields. Now keep straight on down the middle of a field aiming for a wall corner and passing a dewpond on the left. Cross the wall stile to follow the wall close on the left up to and over the stile in the field corner.

5. {E} Turn left along the Limestone Way. Follow the winding track, ignoring tracks and paths on the left. After about a mile you pass through a gate to start the gradual descent into Miller's Dale.

6. Soon you will walk behind a house, go through a farm gate, cross a concrete drive, and turn right, signed Limestone Way. {F} Keep straight on to join a stony track, going through a gate and eventually joining the road.

7. Turn right down the minor road to join the B6049 in Miller's Dale. {G} Continue in the same direction for a few metres, then turn left down steps. Turn left again to follow the No Through Road sign to Litton.

8. In a mile and having passed the entrance to the Youth Hostel leave the road to turn sharp left just after the No Public Parking at Litton Mill. {H}

9. Walk up the very peaceful dale for nearly a mile back to the car park and picnic area. In one stretch of the dale you can walk on either side of the stream. There are a number of conveniently placed benches and some interesting wood sculptures. {I}

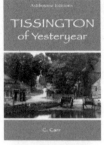

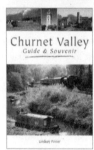